FESTUS ADEYEYE

21 DAYS PRAYER DEVOTIONAL
for a Life of Unlimited Manifestations

21 Days Prayer Devotional for a Life of Unlimited Manifestations

Copyright © 2019 by Festus Adeyeye

Printed in the United States of America. All rights reserved solely by the author. No part of this book may be reproduced in any form without the written permission of the author.

Unless otherwise indicated, Bible quotations are taken from King James Version. Copyright © 1988 by B. B. Kirkbride Bible Company. Encarta World English Dictionary 1998 - 2004 Microsoft Corporation.

ISBN 13: 978-1-7343991-2-7

EDITED BY: Titilola A. Akinyemi

PUBLISHED BY: Platform for Success Press

+1 917 826 3566, press@platformforsuccess.org

ORDERING INFORMATION:

To order books and tapes by Festus Adeyeye, please write to:

Festus Adeyeye

Adeyeye Evangelistic Ministries (AEM)

P.O. Box 810,

West Hempstead, NY 11552

E-mail: adevministries@gmail.com

TABLE OF CONTENTS

Introduction 5

Daily Prayer Guide For Morning & Evening Devotion 13

Day 1 - Enough Is Enough 19

Day 2 - I Am Fruitful And Not Barren 23

Day 3 - Overcoming Obstacles To Your Fruitfulness 29

Day 4 - Unlocking A Locked Destiny 35

Day 5 - It Is My Time To Move Forward 41

Day 6 - As Far As You Can See 47

Day 7 - I Am Free Indeed 53

Day 8 - Arise And Be Healed 59

Day 9 - How To Secure Divine Help 65

Day 10 - Wisdom - Your Power Into The World Of Unlimited Manifestations 73

Day 11 - Living A Life Of Impact 77

Day 12 - Engaging The Voice Of God For Unlimited Manifestations 85

Day 13 - I Am Authorized For Financial Abundance 93

Day 14 - I Am Restored By Covenant 99

Day 15 - I Shall Eat The Good Of The Land 105

Day 16 - Rising Above The Limitations Of Life For A New Level Of Results 111

Day 17 - I Embrace Direction For My Manifestations 119

Day 18 - This Is My New Day: My Season Of Newness 125

Day 19 - I Receive Grace To Conquer Worry And Anxiety 133

Day 20 - All Things Are Now Ready: My Season Of Supernatural Provision 141

Day 21 - I Am Positioned For Unlimited Harvest: Through Thanksgiving 147

Daily Breakthrough Prayer Points 155

The Greatest Prayer Of All Time 161

INTRODUCTION

SEASON OF UNLIMITED MANIFESTATIONS

Welcome to your season of unlimited manifestations. It is not a season to be hidden; it is not your season to be limited; and it is not your season to be obscured. This is your season of unhindered manifestations. Inside every boy is a great man, and inside every girl is a great woman. So also, inside of you is the man or woman of exploits. This material is thus set to bring a lasting transformation in you that will birth great manifestations. It is a divine journey meant to release you into a whole new level of spiritual experience. You may not be changed in the presence of man, but you are guaranteed a change in the presence of God.

2 Corinthians 3:18. But we all, with open face beholding as in a glass the glory of the Lord, are changed into the same image from glory to glory, even as by the Spirit of the Lord.

As you behold God through his words, you are changed into the glory of those words. The truth is, you become what and who you behold. Prayerfully go through this material and allow the Holy Spirit to produce the appropriate change in your life.

Every bird is born to fly, and every fish is born to swim. Likewise, every child of God is born a star and a wonder; a pacesetter and a trailblazer. You were born to rule the world in your field. You were born for divine manifestations and the achievement of unusual accomplishments. Essentially, God created everybody with value.

WHAT DOES "MANIFESTATION" MEAN?

1. The word "manifestation" is the Greek word "phanerosis," which means to make visible or to show forth or to make known. There is a time to be hidden and there is a time to be made manifest.

   Luke 1:80. So the child grew and became strong in spirit, and was in the deserts till the day of his manifestation to Israel.

   1 Peter 2:9. Gideon moved from being a coward hiding in a cave to manifesting the power of God in his generation, destroyed the altar of darkness and led the nation in national repentance.

   God's intention is to show you to the world. You are not an accident waiting to happen, you are a miracle on your way to be made manifest.

2. It means to be visibly used by God on the earth.

   Romans 8:19. For the earnest expectation of the creature waiteth for the manifestation of the sons of God.

   The people on the earth are crying out for the exploits of the sons of God. The world is waiting to see and receive the "revelation of the sons of God," which Jesus has given to each one of us as the son of God. God has given you a song, a dream, a revelation; and the world is waiting for it. There is a dimension of God that only you has been divinely endowed to manifest; it will bring joy to the joyless, hope to the hopeless, peace to the troubled, and liberty to the oppressed. The destinies of many are intertwined with your own destiny. Their fulfillment is directly connected to your level of manifestation. The people of this world are suffering from diseases, loneliness, poverty, and curses; some are hooked on alcohol and narcotics; some are suffering from depression, emotional pain, and feelings of rejection. They are all waiting for your manifestations and mine.

3. Manifestation occurs when you stop living as a victim of generational limitations, and become a generational asset. You are excluded from whatever generational limitations and wickedness are operating in your family, and you begin to make generational impact. No matter how dark it is in the world, you are not permitted to be swallowed by the darkness.

Isaiah 60:1-3. Arise, shine; for thy light is come, and the glory of the LORD is risen upon thee. For, behold, the darkness shall cover the earth, and gross darkness the people: but the LORD shall arise upon thee, and his glory shall be seen upon thee. And the Gentiles shall come to thy light, and kings to the brightness of thy rising.

4. Manifestation, is operating in dominion.

One of the ways to experience unlimited manifestations is accessing the presence of God through learning. That is, accessing the presence of God by divine encounter with the truth of his word and the Holy Spirit. Therefore I urge you to prayerfully read and study this material with the attitude of a learner and with an attitude of humility.

Jesus said in *Matthew 11:28-29, Come to Me, all you who labor and are heavy laden, and I will give you rest. Take My yoke upon you and learn from Me, for I am gentle and lowly in heart, and you will find rest for your souls.*

Many have been living with burdens, fear, and repressions, but there is a divine readiness to release you from such, today. The antidote to a life of stress, fear and oppression is the presence of

God. The presence of God will literally remove and shatter burdens. It was once said that one of the most prescribed medications in America is Valium, which relaxes muscles in order to help people deal with stress. We live in an uptight, stressed out, anxiety-ridden culture, today. So as you come daily meditating with this resource, do so with the attitude someone expecting to encounter God's presence.

There is a supernatural rest that only comes from the presence of God. It is the rest that money cannot buy. This rest is not cessation from activity but rather, peace within the activities and challenges of life; peace that gives one the ability to rest, circumstances notwithstanding. This kind of rest refreshes and revitalizes. It shatters yoke and lifts burdens. However, this rest comes only by learning from Jesus. It requires having a desire to learn, the readiness to know and embrace the truth, and an attitude of humility. You must be open to what God will say to you, at all times.

Being violent in the spirit is also a necessity. Life does not give you what you deserve; life gives you what you demand. Aggressive Christianity is the key to progressive living.

Matthew 11:12. And from the days of John the Baptist until now the kingdom of heaven suffereth violence, and the violent take it by force.

Do not be complacent; do not allow the devil to wreak havoc in your life. You must passionately press for the change and the renewal of your destiny. If Satan succeeds in reducing your passion, he has succeeded in robbing you of your next level breakthrough. Be passionate about where you are going. Wherever you have failed in the past, this is your season to arise and press for a change. *Micah 7:8.* Breakthroughs are the deliberate acts of God as provoked by the deliberate acts of men. God wants you to develop a holy anger this month, against whatever aspect of your life that is not in line with redemption. You shall see the full restoration of your glorious destiny, in Jesus name.

PRAY UNTIL SOMETHING HAPPENS [PUSH]

This is the season to pray until something happens (PUSH) That is, you must be persistent in the place of prayer. To PUSH is to be tenacious in the place of prayer, praying until you receive answers to your prayer requests. Persistence is required for prayers to be answered. You must have a tenacious attitude and refuse to give up until you manifest. So importunity is not an act of unbelief but a proof of persistence, steadfastness, and prevailing faith in prayer.

Luke 11:5-13. And he said unto them, Which of you shall have a friend, and shall go unto him at midnight, and say unto him, Friend, lend me three loaves; For a friend of mine in his journey is come to me, and I have nothing to set before him? And he from within shall answer and say, Trouble me not: the door is now shut, and my children are with me in bed; I cannot rise and give thee. I say unto you, Though he will not rise and give him, because he is his friend, yet because of his importunity he will rise and give him as many as he needeth. And I say unto you, Ask, and it shall be given you; seek, and ye shall find; knock, and it shall be opened unto you. For every one that asketh receiveth; and he that seeketh findeth; and to him that knocketh it shall be opened. If a son shall ask bread of any of you that is a father, will he give him a stone? or if he ask a fish, will he for a fish give him a serpent? Or if he shall ask an egg, will he offer him a scorpion? If ye then, being evil, know how to give good gifts unto your children: how much more shall your heavenly Father give the Holy Spirit to them that ask him?

No matter the dispensational changes on the earth prayer is still one of the answers for breakthrough. Prayer has the possibility to affect everything that affects us. *James 5:16-18.* Prayer guarantees open heaven; it was a major secret in the life of Jesus. *Luke 11.* There are several benefits to praying and the refusal to pray is to unknowingly make your destiny, and that of those associated with you, a prey of the enemy. *Luke 18:1. Matthew 26:41.* Prayer subdues the kingdom of darkness. *Ephesians 6:12-18.* To refuse to pray is to sentence your destiny to a life without peace, full of worry and anxiety. *Philippians 4:6-7.* Prayer brings a divine glow to a destiny. To refuse to pray is to reduce your life to an ordinary existence without a divine touch.

Why Push?

1. For every prophecy, you have to war it out. You do not watch out for a prophecy; you wage war until it comes to reality. *Deuteronomy 2:24.* Hold prayer vigils over everything God has told you, praying over them diligently. Elijah received the word, spoke the word to Ahab, and then prayed for them to manifest. He prayed seven times until the manifestations came.
2. Satan is prepared to resist all of your open doors and blessings from God. *1 Corinthians 16:9.* Hence, if you are not ready to contend in battle, you may not obtain what belongs to you. Between desire and delivery, there are obstacles that must be overcome. The host of darkness contending against the answers to your prayers must be overcome and subdued. *Ephesians 6:12-18. Daniel 10.*

You do not wish problems away. Rise up to that challenge. Do not give up until the answers come. Do not fold your hands and watch that situation persist, because there is no possession without contention. If there is any drought around you, do not wait for the rain; pray it down.

How Do I Push?

1. The end must be settled in your mind from the beginning. Elijah already declared the outcome to Ahab even before he started the prayer.
2. *Mark 11:24. Therefore I say unto you, What things whatsoever ye desire, when ye pray, believe that ye receive them, and ye shall have them.*
3. Refuse to look at the contradictory evidence. Elijah placed his face between his knees. The widow in Luke 18 refused to take no, for an answer. Take your focus off the circumstances. *Romans 4:17-21.*
4. *Ecclesiastes 11:4. He who observes the wind will not sow, and he who regards the clouds will not reap.*
5. Be persistent with praise. *Romans 4:17-21.*
6. Ensure that your prayers are scriptural.

NECESSITY FOR PREVAILING PRAYER

1. *Matthew 17:21 - Howbeit this kind goes not out but by prayer and fasting.* There are some situations that are stubborn and will require spiritual tenacity on your part. Acts 12:5. The church recognized that a prevailing prayer was necessary in order to deliver Peter's destiny from the oppressive hand of Herod who had purposed to kill him. Peter's destiny was liberated and rescued from the clutches of death because the church prayed ceaselessly. This is your hour to stay focused and unflinching so you can break away from the grip of anything holding your back from experiencing the abundant life, in Jesus name.
2. Prevailing prayer is necessary when your expected desire seems to be delayed.

    1st Kings 18:41-44 - And Elijah said unto Ahab, Get thee up, eat and drink; for there is a sound of abundance of rain. So Ahab went up to eat and to drink. And Elijah went up to the top of Carmel; and he cast himself down upon the earth, and put his face between his knees, And said to his servant, Go up now, look toward the sea. And he went up, and looked, and said, there is nothing. And he said, Go again seven times. And it came to pass at the seventh time, that he said, Behold, there ariseth a little cloud out of the sea, like a man's hand. And he said, Go up, say unto Ahab, Prepare thy chariot, and get thee down, that the rain stop thee not.

Elijah positioned his face between his knees and refused to look at external situations. He continued in prayer, until heaven responded to his decree. You too must be ready to pray until something happens. Do not allow any setback on the journey to discourage you. The next 21 days and beyond require your intense focus and absolute dependency on the person of the Holy Spirit for help and guidance.

DAILY PRAYER GUIDE FOR MORNING & EVENING DEVOTION

MORNING DEVOTION PLAN

Psalm 100:1-5 -*(A Psalm of praise.) Make a joyful noise unto the LORD, all ye lands. Serve the LORD with gladness: come before his presence with singing. Know ye that the LORD he [is] God: [it is] he [that] hath made us, and not we ourselves; [we are] his people, and the sheep of his pasture. Enter into his gates with thanksgiving, [and] into his courts with praise: be thankful unto him, [and] bless his name. For the LORD [is] good; his mercy [is] everlasting; and his truth [endureth] to all generations.*

Psalm 5:3 - *My voice shalt thou hear in the morning, O LORD; in the morning will I direct* my prayer *unto thee, and will look up.*

Psalm 34:5 - *Those who look up to him will be radiant with joy, no shadow of shame will darken their faces.*

2nd Corinthians 3:18. *But we all, with open face beholding as in a glass the glory of the Lord, are changed into the same image from glory to glory, even as by the Spirit of the Lord.*

The way each day will look to you begins with whom you behold daily. No man will be able to despise your if you see God's face daily before you see the face of men.

Note:

- Give the Holy Spirit the freedom in leading you and do not be too rigid and mechanical in praying.
- You can pray each prayer item many times before moving to the next, as the Holy Spirit leads you.

- In addition, make use of the prayer points that are listed at the end of each day's devotional.

Begin your day by singing praises unto the Lord. Being alive is a privilege and not an entitlement.

Enter into His presence with thanksgiving and with praise. Be thankful unto Him and bless His name, for His goodness and mercy that keeps you, daily. Sing any praise or worship song that the Holy Spirit brings to your mind. Sing also in the spirit (tongue).

Declare that the Lord is God; that He is the one who has made you, and that you are His child, the apple of His eyes. Declare that this is the day the Lord has made and that you will rejoice and be glad in it.

Romans 8:26. The Holy Spirit is your indwelling prayer partner. At the beginning of every prayer time, invite Him to energize, strengthen, and empower you, as follows:

"I now by faith commit my prayer time into the hands of the Holy Spirit; I hereby yield my WILL, my INTELLECT, my MIND, my EMOTIONS, and my VOCAL CORDS, to the Holy Spirit. I thank you Holy Spirit for helping me to pray the will of God concerning my life, effectively and diligently."

Rebuke any form of distraction; rebuke early morning heaviness, confusion, worry, depression or any hangover resulting from bad dreams. Cancel any spirit of procrastination that may want you to postpone this prayer time.

Prayerfully ask God for the forgiveness of your sins and ask for the blood of Jesus to cleanse you.

Pray Lamentations 3:22-23 and pray in the Holy Ghost as led. Pray that God in His mercy will make your prayer hour fruitful and effective.

Pray with the DAILY BREAKTHROUGH PRAYER POINTS on Page 155.

Closing Prayer for Morning Devotion

I thank you Holy Spirit, for being my indwelling prayer partner. As I conclude my morning session I thank you that my mind is alert; I am focused on the things from above, and my mind is focused on profitable things. I thank you for reminding me and giving me the ability to pray effectively in the evening.

EVENING DEVOTIONAL PLAN

Come with a concentrated focus to be blessed. Commit this prayer hour to the Holy Spirit and ask for His strength, guidance and grace. Romans 8:26. Pray each prayer item many times before moving to the next one.

Heavenly father, I thank and worship your wonderful name for all you have done for me and my entire family today. I thank you for the things you are doing now and the things you will do.

Sing praise and worship songs to bless God and fellowship with Him as you are led now.

Lord, I ask for your forgiveness in any way I have sinned against you today in my words, deeds and actions, I ask that you cleanse me with the blood of Jesus.

Lord, I commit this night into your hands. I ask that you give your angels charge over me and my family to guide and protect us in Jesus name.

Heavenly father, I pray by the authority in the name of Jesus for the restoration of every good thing that I lost today. I declare that

I will eat in plenty and be satisfied and will praise the Lord. I pray that you will restore my joy, anointing, favor, promotion and every good opportunity lost in Jesus name.

I soak myself and my entire household in the blood of Jesus and I come against every evil dream, every attack of the enemy and nightmares concerning my family and my ministry in Jesus name.

Tonight, I take authority and dominion over every plan of the witches, wizards and all agents of darkness in Jesus name. None of their weapons fashioned against me shall prosper.

Pray about any painful issue or incident that happened today and is threatening your peace. Place it in God's hands and rest on Him. Receive peace now. Isaiah 26:3.

Lay your hands on your head now and begin blessing your entire life. Decree the blessings of the Lord over your life.

My head rejects shame this year and beyond. I choose glory and not shame. I choose to shine. I choose to lend and not borrow. I choose to rejoice and not sorrow. I choose to live and not die in Jesus name.

I cover myself, my family, my relations, and friends, with the blood of Jesus.

I soak this house and all properties in my entire neighborhood in the blood of Jesus and I forbid the activities of agents of darkness in Jesus name.

Lord, build a wall of fire around my life, family, job, academics, business, career and ministry tonight in Jesus name.

Lord, I thank you for causing my spirit to be violent against the spirit of darkness in my sleep and dream(s).

Lord, I ask that you be with me and reveal strategies and wisdom for progress and restoration unto me in my dream(s) tonight in Jesus name.

Thank you Lord because you give your beloved sleep. I will sleep peacefully without any nightmare and I will wake up strong and revitalized in Jesus name.

I thank you Lord for waking me up in the night by the help of the Holy Spirit and thank you for enabling me to pray fervently and to study your word with understanding, in Jesus name.

[You may repeat any of these points again now, or you can include other prayer points, as you are led].

Day 1

ENOUGH IS ENOUGH

DAY 1
ENOUGH IS ENOUGH

Deuteronomy 2:3 And the LORD spake unto me, saying, Ye have compassed this mountain long enough: turn you northward.

This is your season to arise and enforce your turnaround. I can hear the spirit of the Lord saying, "enough is enough."

What are the situations in your life that have festered for so long? This is the day to say to them: enough is enough. This is the day to arise and leverage the power of prayer. God told the Israelites in the above scriptures; "You have compassed this mountain for too long." For whatsoever mountain-like situations that seem immoveable, and seem to resist your efforts and prayers, this is the day for a turnaround.

Just like God spoke to Pharaoh through Moses, saying, "Let My People Go" (see Exodus 9:1), God is saying once again; "enough is enough." Therefore, whatever is holding your destiny down must let you go.

Enough is enough. Enough of sleepless nights. I am declaring by the Word of the Lord that the seasons are changing!

One fact about challenges of life is that no challenge is meant to last forever. Every challenge has an expiry date.

Day 1 - Enough Is Enough

Proverbs 23:18. Surely there is an end and the expectation of the righteous shall not be cut off.

One of the keys to enforcing a change is to develop a holy anger. It is getting to a point where you are done with the status quo; where you develop an expectation for the change you want to see. This is because it is your expectation that determines the end. It is your expectation that draws the line. The end is determined not only by God, but by your expectations. The time you connect becomes your own time. The day you encounter him by faith is your day. It was on the platform of "enough is enough" in Shiloh that Hannah became a mother of children. *1 Samuel 1:9-13.*

It was the driving force behind the faith movement of blind Bartimaeus that made him persist for a change of story. *Mark 10:46.* As Jesus passed by Jericho that very day, every blind person in town had the opportunity for a miracle, but only blind Bartimaeus experienced his own miracle. There was no particular blind person scheduled to be healed on that day; only blind Bartimaeus was desperate enough. Breakthroughs are the deliberate acts of God as provoked by the deliberate acts of men.

Your expectation must be rooted in knowing that God is not just about to prepare what will guarantee your change; he already prepared everything required for your moment of change, at Redemption. *Romans 8:32.*

Identify what must end today. As you go through the day, leverage the power of redemption in prayers to see an end to longstanding issues in your life.

I am convinced that you will sing a new song over those issues.

Day 1: *Victorious thought for the day.* You can never possess what you do not pursue, and whatever you tolerate, you cannot change.

PRAYERS

Proverbs 23:18. By the authority of God's word, I decree an end to every unpleasant situation in my life. I command a total turnaround for good, in my health, in my family, in my career and in every area of my life in Jesus name.

John 19:30. When he had received the drink, Jesus said, "It is finished." With that, he bowed his head and gave up his spirit. By the finished work of Calvary, I say to sickness in my life; it is finished. I say to poverty in my life; it is finished. I say to barrenness in my life; it is finished. I say to the operation and oppression of the devil in my life; it is finished. From today and henceforth, I begin to walk in the fullness of divine favor, liberty and good health, by the authority in the name of Jesus.

Day 2

I AM FRUITFUL AND NOT BARREN

DAY 2
I AM FRUITFUL AND NOT BARREN

Welcome to your day and season of fruitfulness. This is the day to leverage your covenant privileges to shatter barrenness and embrace a life of fruitfulness. God's mandate for you today and always is to be fruitful. God is against barrenness in whatever form. Living a life of barrenness is contrary to covenant. Barrenness and fruitlessness contradict the first word God spoke to mankind in *Genesis 1:28. And God blessed them, and God said unto them, Be fruitful, and multiply, and replenish the earth, and subdue it: and have dominion over the fish of the sea, and over the fowl of the air, and over every living thing that moveth upon the earth.*

WHAT DOES IT MEAN TO BE FRUITFUL?

It means to produce good, beneficial, and profitable results. It means to produce fruit in abundance. It also refers to productiveness and fertility. God's desire is for you to be fruitful in every area of your life. There are five different areas of fruitfulness where God has blessed and empowered you, and in which you are expected to be fruitful.

1. The Fruit of your body [Physical productivity]. This involves your health and fertility. By covenant, you are guaranteed the blessing of fruitfulness in the fruit of your

womb. *Psalm 127: 3.* As such barrenness will be terminated in your life, in Jesus name.

2. The Fruit of the mind [Ideas]. *Jeremiah 6:19.* When God made Adam, he did not give him a bed, soap, toothpaste, or a knife, He just said, "be fruitful." Adam had to engage his mind and find ways to extract everything he needed from his environment. If you look closely, by Genesis Chapter 4 which was only seven generations after Adam, amazing things had been achieved. They had found ways to make tents and raise livestock; they manufactured musical instruments and crafted implements of iron and bronze. Without having gone to school, how did they learn the concept of music and how did they learn to craft a harp, attaching each string at a different tension in order to create different notes? *Job 32: 8* gives us an insight, telling us, *"But there is a spirit in man and the breath of the Almighty gives him understanding."* For this reason, a lack of education can never be an excuse for not being fruitful. As a child of God, you have the mind of God. You have the mind of creativity. Ideas rule the world. You are to transform and rule the world through consecrated and anointed ideas. There is an idea in you for which the world is craving. *Philemon 14. But without thy mind would I do nothing. Genesis 11:6.* Think productive thoughts. Feed your mind with things that edify.

3. Fruit of the mouth [Words]. Proverbs 18: 20-21. A man's belly shall be satisfied with the fruit of his mouth: and with the increase of his lips shall he be filled. Death and life are in the power of the tongue: and they that love it shall eat the fruit thereof. Words can be productive or destructive. We exercise dominion for fruitfulness through the words that we speak. Our words have impact in three realms; it compels satanic opposition, it initiates the angels, and it also causes heaven to act on our behalf. 2 Corinthians 4:8-

9, 13. Even at times of difficulty, you need to keep speaking and confessing that God is at work in your life.

Speaking the word of God with your mouth is one of the greatest weapons you have against the devil and against any circumstance. *Psalms 103:20. Bless the LORD, ye his angels that excel in strength, that do his commandments, hearkening unto the voice of his word.* Remember that Jesus said that we will give account for any idle (useless, barren or inactive) words that we speak (*Matt 12: 36*) and therefore, I challenge you to determine that you will refuse to speak idle or destructive words. The words that you store in your heart produce the fruit of your mouth. *Joel 3:10: Let the weak say I am strong.*

4. Fruit of the hands [Work]. As a redeemed child of God, you have been endowed to be fruitful in whatever you do with your hands. There are some who labor and do not see any result because their hands have been cursed. *Proverbs 31: 30-31. Isaiah 62:8-9.* You should begin to work creatively, diligently, and tirelessly. *Isaiah 3:10 say ye to the righteous, that it shall be well with him: for they shall eat the fruit of his doings.*
5. Fruit of the Spirit [Character]. *Galatians 5: 22-23.* So, this is your season to be fruitful in your body, in your mind, your mouth, your hands, and your spirit.

Pray today that God should plant the dream and vision for your fruitfulness in your heart. Pray against every form of unfruitfulness and barrenness; be it foundational, personal, or conveyed by people.

Day 2: *Victorious thought for the day.* Everything reproduces after its own kind and since I am an offspring of Jehovah God who is forever fruitful, barrenness is contrary to my DNA. I am fruitful and cannot be barren.

PRAYERS

By the authority in the name of Jesus, I plead the blood of Jesus over the foundation of my life to cleanse me of any root of barrenness.

By the power of divine connection with God as a branch to the fruitful vine; I draw grace for unlimited fruitfulness in Jesus name

From today and henceforth, I shall be fruitful in my body. I shall be fruitful in the works of my hand. I shall produce fruitful ideas, and wisdom and insights in my mind. I shall be fruitful in the words of my mouth and I shall be fruitful in my spirit.

Day 3

OVERCOMING OBSTACLES TO YOUR FRUITFULNESS

DAY 3
OVERCOMING OBSTACLES TO YOUR FRUITFULNESS

Genesis 1:28. And God blessed them, and God said unto them, Be fruitful, and multiply, and replenish the earth, and subdue it: and have dominion over the fish of the sea, and over the fowl of the air, and over every living thing that moveth upon the earth.

This is your covenant day to rise above obstacles to your fruitfulness. Although it is your mandate to be fruitful by redemption, there are factors that must be overcome for a life of continuous fruitfulness. Today is devoted to knowing and overcoming the factors that resist fruitfulness.

OBSTACLES TO FRUITFULNESS

1. **Excuses.** Excuse in any form is a killer of progress and fruitfulness. Whenever you give excuses, you give up your power to change and improve. Excuses are demonic suggestions for enslaving and entrapping your destiny.
2. **People's opinion.** *Mark 10:48.* This is allowing what people are saying about you to hinder your positive actions. Blind Bartimaeus did not allow the negative opinion of people to stop his move towards his progress. You must deal with the fact that everybody will not like you, and

you must make up your mind not to surrender your destiny to noisy negatives. Hang around those who will push you to your destiny. Stop worrying about what negative people will say. You must die to self. If you are going to be fruitful, you must die to people's opinion, since some people do not mind you shining, as long you do not outshine them.

3. **Discouragement.** Discouragement is the loss of confidence or enthusiasm in the pursuit of your destiny either as a result of opposition or the normal process of life. Discouragement is a robber of destiny. This usually happens when things do not go as planned. David and his men were known to be men of valor, and men of courage and determination. However, the incident in *1 Samuel* 30 affected them so much, that they were greatly distressed and discouraged. Nothing they did seemed to work in their favor. But God's plan for their lives had not changed. Weeping is not the plan of God. To throw in the towel is also not the plan of God.

4. **Fear**. Fear in any form paralyzes initiative. It stiffens growth and fruitfulness. It stops progress and destroys our confidence in God. As Kenneth Copeland said, "fear tolerated, is faith contaminated." Fear is the most potent negative force on the earth. Fear of failure, fear of the unknown, fear of death, and fear of opposition. The worst is the fear of failure. Pray for the courage to trust God no matter what. *Hebrews 10:35*. Courage is not the absence of fear; it is learning to confront your fear with the reality of God's presence. This is your hour to break free from any form of fear. In order to embrace your fruitfulness, you must stand in faith, focusing on the ability and the strength of Jehovah God. What wrong verdict have you been given? Fear not. Irrespective of the challenges you will be confronted with, trust and depend on God to do

what he says he would do. Stand on the authority of his word; stand still, and let God arise and fight your battle.

5. **Comparison.** When God made you he made the best. One of the killers of fruitfulness is comparison. The man with one talent failed to be fruitful because his focus was on what God gave others rather than on maximizing his own resources. You have been uniquely made, uniquely gifted and uniquely packaged for a glorious destiny. God placed all that you need inside of you, for your fruitfulness. Stop looking at the greener grass on the other side.

6. **Prayerlessness.** One of the keys responsible for a fruitful destiny is consistent prayer. Prayer was one of the engines that drove the destiny of Jesus Christ. *Luke 3:21, Luke 6:12-13, Luke 9:28, Mark 6:46. And when he had sent them away, he departed into a mountain to pray. And when even was come, the ship in the midst of the sea. He walked upon eh sea. John 18:1.* Prayer helps to overcome opposition to your destiny. Many destinies are dried up and fruitless through prayerlessness. *Nehemiah 4:4, 9.* Nehemiah prayed all along to overcome obstacles to his vision. Prayerfulness turns your battle to God's battle. It turns over your struggles and battles to God. Prayer moves you beyond people and spirits.

Apply yourself diligently to the fulfilment of your destiny and avoid self-sabotaging behaviors. Make up your mind to be diligent in whatever you do.

Ecclesiastes 10:15. When in doubt, seek to know how to get things done. Ignorance is not bliss. What and who do I need to get to where I am going?

Proverbs 10:4 (NKJV). He who has a slack hand becomes poor, but the hand of the diligent makes rich.

Proverbs 22:29 (NLT). Do you see any truly competent workers? They will serve kings rather than working for ordinary people.

Blind Bartimaeus overcame the barriers to his fruitfulness through his passionate pursuit of his desired miracle. No matter the obstacles in your way today, let there be a passionate and an unstoppable drive to overcome. Jesus secured your fruitfulness and has given you the victory over all the oppositions of life. *1 Corinthians 15:57. But thanks be to God, which giveth us the victory through our Lord Jesus Christ.*

Day 3: *Victorious thought for the day.* By the redemptive work of Jesus Christ on the cross, my destiny is unstoppable. *Romans 8:31.*

PRAYERS

I reject and break down any form of mental barrier, physical barrier, spiritual barrier, self-imposed barrier and satanic barrier, that is hindering my fruitfulness in Jesus name.

Every siege standing against the advancement of my destiny is shattered in the name of Jesus.

Every alliance and conspiracy against my fruitfulness is destroyed in the name of Jesus.

Day 4

UNLOCKING A LOCKED DESTINY

DAY 4
UNLOCKING A LOCKED DESTINY

This is your set time for the fulfilment of destiny. This is your day of liberty and freedom from any form of bondage. Whether the devil likes it or not, whether your enemies like it or not; there is a specific day, month, and year that your story will change, and the good news is that that time is now. In several instances in the bible you read the phrase, "And it came to pass." Your dreams shall become realities in Jesus name. Your imprisonments shall turn to freedom in Jesus name. What are you believing God for? A new job, healing, a baby, prosperity, new accommodation? They shall all come to pass. The story of your life will change by the power that changed the story of Lazarus from the grave to life. It shall come to pass that you shall come out of the grave, and arise, and shine in Jesus name.

Whatsoever you see in the physical is actually a copy of the things in the spirit. Just as you have doors in the physical, so there are doors in the spiritual. Your actual experiences in life are determined by the doors opened to you in the spiritual realm. There are several Christians operating under a closed destiny. You can have two people selling the same product, and one prospers while the other does not. Two people may work in similar positions, and one's career advances, while the other's does not, all due to a locked destiny. Every location, business, opportunity, etc., summed up in destiny, has a door. Until your destiny is unlocked, you cannot be a blessing to your generation.

WHAT ARE THE SIGNS OF A LOCKED DESTINY?

1. Every door that opens naturally for others becomes closed when it is your turn.
2. When you discover that logically, you qualify for a position or benefit, but you are denied for no justifiable reason. You attend interviews consistently, but there are no positive outcomes.
3. When your destiny is locked, circumstances and situations react against you. Hence, life becomes hostile, bitter, nasty, or unconducive for you. Things that should take a short period of time to happen take years for you.
4. 4. Your destiny is locked, when someone is trying to help you, all of a sudden and mysteriously, the assistance is no longer forthcoming.

WHAT ARE THE EVIDENCES OF AN UNLOCKED DESTINY?

After 37 years of imprisonment, king Jehoiachin was released from prison, and given a seat above the seats of the kings in Babylon. His prison garments were removed, and subsequently, he ate regularly at the king's table and enjoyed a regular allowance according to his daily needs, for the rest of his life. *2 Kings 25:27-30*. His locked destiny was unlocked.

When your destiny is unlocked, God and life, give you something memorable. Memorial blessings become yours. You begin to enjoy unforgettable breakthroughs. The destiny of Abraham was unlocked the day God instructed him to get out of his father's house That was the day his captivity ended, and his destiny opened up for a generational blessing.

When your destiny is unlocked, impossibilities of past years suddenly become a testimony. Right from his birth, everything worked against Jacob. Jacob labored for seven years so he could marry Rachel, but they gave him Leah. Jacob married Racheal after another seven years, but her womb was closed until God remembered him in *Genesis 30:22*.

Joseph became number eleven instead of number one. He became the object of ancestral exchange. Even at number 11, everything that would have favored him did not work; but a day came in Peniel, when the impossibilities of past years became a testimony. Joseph had been in prison for years. It was a story of one problem after another. From taking food to his brothers, to finding himself in a waterless pit, to been sold in slavery, to becoming a slave, to becoming a prisoner. However, a day came when the losses of past years turned to profit. Joseph got the prime minister's job without any political affiliation; without being a citizen of that country; and as an ex-convict. He was brought out of prison, sworn-in, and got married, all in one day. Joseph's story can be best described as a locked destiny that was unlocked. *Genesis 41:37-40*

When your destiny is unlocked, you begin to enjoy divine remembrances. When the destiny of Mordecai was unlocked, his past labor and efforts that had gone unrewarded were suddenly recollected. The book of remembrance was opened, and he enjoyed honor and lifting. *Esther 6:1-8*. The years of barrenness came to an end in the life of Racheal when her destiny opened up. *Genesis 30:22. And God remembered Rachel, and God hearkened to her, and opened her womb.* I see your destiny opened up for unlimited manifestations in Jesus name.

When your destiny is unlocked, stagnation gives way to progress. *Genesis 41:40-46*. When your destiny is unlocked, the law of nature will be suspended for you. Usual procedures are upended, as seen in the story of David, when he was to be anointed king. Samuel said he would not stop enquiring from the LORD, until he anointed the right person to the throne.

HOW DO I UNLOCK MY DESTINY?

1. Get out of sin. (Satan's Identity Number). Sin is a destiny blocker. Step out of sin today and step into grace. *John 1:12.*
2. Develop a hunger for an encounter with God. Jacob's destiny opened up when he pressed for an encounter at Peniel. Your dependency should be solely on God, and not on people and thing.
   Genesis 32:27-31. And he said unto him, What is thy name? And he said, Jacob. And he said, Thy name shall be called no more Jacob, but Israel: for as a prince hast thou power with God and with men, and hast prevailed. And Jacob asked him, and said, Tell me, I pray thee, thy name. And he said, Wherefore is it that thou dost ask after my name? And he blessed him there. And Jacob called the name of the place Peniel: for I have seen God face to face, and my life is preserved. And as he passed over Penuel the sun rose upon him, and he halted upon his thigh.
3. Pray your destiny out of any containment. Men ought always to pray and not to faint. *Luke 18.*
4. Your financial seed-faith giving can unlock your destiny. It was the seed of burnt offerings that Solomon gave that unlocked his destiny. *2 Kings 3.* It was the seed Hannah vowed that unlocked her destiny. *1 Samuel 1:11.* It was the seed of obedience in readiness to sacrifice Isaac that unlocked the destiny of Abraham. It was the seed of hospitality of accommodating the prophet that opened up the destiny of the woman in *2 Kings 4:8.*

Day 4: *Victorious thought for the day.* When God opens, no one can shut, and when he shuts, no one can open. Since God has the key of life, no power is strong enough to lock my destiny.

PRAYERS

Heavenly Father, I decree by your word that everything you have not spoken over my life that is having a negative effect, is cancelled in Jesus name. *Lamentations 3:37.*

Every curse spoken over my life is shattered by the power of your word in Jesus name.

By the authority of God's word, I command every good door that has closed in my life to be opened, in Jesus name.

Day 5

IT IS MY TIME TO MOVE FORWARD

DAY 5
IT IS MY TIME TO MOVE FORWARD

"When the turn of Esther came…" When, not if. As you pray and meditate on God's word today, it is your turn to go forward. It is your turn to be promoted. It is your turn to experience divine lifting. You will move from grace to grace; from favor to favor; from freedom to freedom, and from lifting to lifting.

As a child of God, if you walk in the fullness of your covenant - then your "turn" is mandatory and not optional, and- your current level will change for the better. You must believe that it is your turn to be remembered for good; your turn to be decorated; and your turn to reign. When God says it is your turn to move forward, there is no one powerful enough to resist it. *Romans 8:31*

Despite the hopeless condition of the Israelites when confronted with the Red Sea in front, the armies of Pharaoh behind them, and mountains around, God saw to it that they moved forward. After about 430 years in captivity and under an oppressive system, God supernaturally delivered them. In just one night, they went from bondage to freedom. They moved from sickness to health. They went from sorrow to joy. They moved from being cursed to being blessed. They moved from poverty to wealth. God brought them forth with silver and gold. *Psalms 105:37*

Genesis 26:12-13. The encounter and experience of Isaac in *Genesis 26* was a destiny fulfilled despite the obstacles. Despite the unfavorable condition and the fierce opposition of the enemy (the Philistines) to stop his progress, God saw to it that Isaac got to his Rehoboth (his place of fruitfulness and unlimited manifestations). He waxed great, went forward and grew until he became very great. *Genesis 26:13.* By the sensing of the spirit, irrespective of where you are or whatever is happening in your life, this is your season to move forward. Your Rehoboth is your place of roominess. It signifies broad and spacious places, and enlargements. It is your place of fruitfulness, fulfillment of the plans of God, and limitless accomplishments, and breakthroughs with no boundaries. *For now hath the Lord made room for us; and we shall be fruitful in the land. Genesis 26:22.*

No matter the level you have attained, there is always a newer dimension of progress. *Proverbs 4:18. Deuteronomy 1:6. Genesis 26:12-13. Then Isaac sowed in that land, and received*

in the same year an hundredfold: and the Lord blessed him. And the man waxed great, and went forward, and grew until he became very great. Isaac experienced four dimensions of progress. He was blessed, he waxed great, he went forward, he grew and became very great. No matter where you are right now, you must know that there is another higher level. To go forward is to forcefully advance, despite opposition. To experience unlimited progress. To increase. To enlarge. You are not permitted to stay on the same spot, counting the same money and fighting the same devil.

Isaiah 60:22 [NKJV]. A little one shall become a thousand, And a small one a strong nation. I, the LORD, will hasten it in its time.

HOW DO I MOVE FORWARD?

Exodus 14:13-15. And Moses said unto the people, Fear ye not, stand still, and see the salvation of the Lord, which he will shew to you today:

for the Egyptians whom ye have seen today, ye shall see them again no more forever. The Lord shall fight for you, and ye shall hold your peace. And the Lord said unto Moses, Wherefore criest thou unto me? speak to the children of Israel, that they go forward:

1. *Exodus 14:13.* Stop being afraid but stand in faith. Fear focuses on the ability and the strength of opposition whereas faith focuses on the ability and the strength of God. Do not surrender your destiny to fear. Your destiny may be attacked, but it is simply because of the size of your testimony. What wrong verdict have you been given? Fear not. Trust and depend on the ability of God to perform his word. Trust God that with him all things are possible. Do not be afraid of tomorrow. Stand still and pray for God to arise and fight your battle. When God arises, the program of the enemy for your life is terminated and your stubborn enemies shall flee. Your wall of Jericho thus collapses.
2. See the Salvation. You need to SEE IT and stand your ground in prayer. God said to Moses, "why are you complaining; see what I want to do." Instead of falling for the intimidation of the enemy, Isaac continued to define his journey. Isaac had a clear vision of what he wanted and where he was going. Stay focused and never give up on your dream. Continue to dream big because they shall all come to pass.
3. Let your determination to succeed be stronger than your enemies' desire to stop you.
4. Stand your ground in prayer. You need to know that life does not give you what you deserve; life gives you what you demand. The Red Sea does not move until you move it. It is never the will of the oppressor to willingly release the oppressed. You do not negotiate with the devil. If you want deliverance and forward movement, you have to speak with command. Your liberty and progress begins

with your voice. *Job 13:19. Who is he that will plead with me? for now, if I hold my tongue, I shall give up the ghost.*

Day 5: *Victorious thought for the day.* I can never have a better yesterday. Each day of my life shall be better, brighter, bigger, fresher, and more prosperous than the previous. *Proverbs 4:18.*

PRAYERS

By the authority in the name of Jesus, I receive the grace to arise and move forward. *1 Samuel 12:6.* Father, advance my destiny by your grace and favor, in the name of Jesus. My father, my father, I receive grace to overcome the human limitations, geographical limitations, family foundation limitations, and spiritual limitations that are keeping me on the same spot, in Jesus name.

Day 6

AS FAR AS YOU CAN SEE

DAY 6
AS FAR AS YOU CAN SEE

Genesis 13:14, 15. And the Lord said unto Abram, after that Lot was separated from him, Lift up thine eyes, and look from the place where thou art northward, and southward, and eastward, and westward: For all the land which thou seest, to thee will I give it, and to thy seed for ever.

The prophetic word for today is engaging your unlimited manifestations through the pursuit of vision. Every person can either see life as good or bad depending on your vision. You can either see abundance or lack. You can either see opportunities or problems. You can either see sickness or health. You can either see blessings or curses. The question to you this day is, "What do you see?" God asked Abraham in the above scripture; *"For all the land which thou seest to thee will I give it and to thy seed forever."* The future you see is the future you will embrace. The future you see, is the future you will feature in. This is because your vision is your future.

The poorest man in life is not the man without money but a man without vision. In fact, a man with money who has no vision will soon become a pauper. The greatest gift God ever gave man is not the gift of sight but the gift of vision. Why? Because sight is a function of the eyes, while vision is a function of the heart. The eyes that look are many, but the eyes that see are few. God never intended for you to live by (eye) sight. Your eyes are the enemies of your vision. Why? Because sight is limited to the capacity of the eyes, but vision is limited to the boundaries of your imagination. Your eyes always show you what is, but vision shows you what could be. Sight restricts you to the present, but vision releases you to the uncharted frontiers of the future.

What is vision? Vision is the capacity to see further than your eyes can look. It is the mental picture of a preferable future. It is possible to be in the midst of chaos and calamity and still experience calmness and peace. You may be broke financially and yet capture a vision for abundance and prosperity. With vision, you will not slumber or die in a slum, even if you were born and raised in such an environment. You can grow up in a slum and still soar higher than eagles. It all depends on *what* you see and *how* you see. People may look at you now and fail to appreciate your person; but as a visionary, let it be known that you are under construction!

Prayerfully develop the ability to see beyond today. *Habakkuk 2:2, 3. And the Lord answered me, and said, Write the vision, and make it plain upon tables, that he may run that readeth it. For the vision is yet for an appointed time, but at the end it shall speak, and not lie: though it tarry, wait for it; because it will surely come, it will not tarry.*

Prayerfully ask God to grant unto you the grace to see his plans, purposes, and mandate for your life. And that your eyes of understanding be opened to know the hidden plans of God for your life. *Ephesians 1:17-19.*

When vision is revealed to you, there are three things to do:
1. Vision must be written. Vision is not just to be in your head, you must document it.
2. Vision must be made clear. The clearer the vision, the easier it is to pursue. Where am I going? How do I get there?

3. You must run with Vision. It is the pursuit of your vision that makes it a reality. It is the pursuit of your vision that takes you from where you are, to where you ought to be. Not just wishes, since "if wishes were horses, beggars would ride.

CHARACTERISTICS OF THE PROTOTYPE OF GOD'S VISION.

1. When it is God's vision, it will inspire you. Inspiration activates; arouses. Even though, it may challenge your faith, it will inspire you.
2. Your vision will change you. In order to fulfill the vision, it will be an adjustment, and a shift in your perspective. Abraham had to forsake tradition; he left his kindred.
3. Your vision will challenge you, to see if you can trust God, even when you cannot see him. God did not give Abraham too much detail. He said, just go and as you go, I will instruct you. You have to believe God and move forward. There is no vision without challenges. When challenges come, begin with thanksgiving and not murmuring. There is always one thing for which you can thank God.
4. Your vision will stretch you. It will provoke your brain to think of new ideas and new strategies. God could just take you today and place you there tomorrow, but he wants you to grow. So, in the course of overcoming challenges, your brain begins to work, and you grow and develop. You do not climb the ladder from the top, but from the bottom. Whenever you try to avoid a process and related challenges, you dodge your future. Whenever you are given a responsibility, it exposes your hidden abilities. The abilities you are not even aware off. Joseph as a slave was given the responsibility to run the palace.

5. Every vision is time-tagged. You need to understand the timing of your life. It was timing that brought Joseph in contact with the baker and the butler. Joseph was forgotten because it was not God's timing. Remembering him earlier would not have been profitable for Joseph. Nothing can stop God's appointed time for you. It was not an error for John the Baptist to be born six months before Jesus. After 430 years of captivity in Egypt, God showed Pharaoh who was in charge. Why timing? He wants you to be prepared. He wants to develop your heart. He wants you to know sometimes, that what is difficult for men is not for him. He wants you to him the praise, and not man.
6. It will be personal, unique, and custom-made for you. His vision for you will fit your person and your ability. *Matthew 25:5*. So do not compare yourself with anyone else. Just do what you can when you can, and let God honor your effort.
7. It will promise a reward of obedience. The reward is to empower and motivate you. *Job 36:11, Isaiah 1:19*. Everything with God is always contingent on obedience.
8. God's vision is always long term. God's vision will keep expanding. After we have fully developed at one level, there is always another level above. There is no end or retirement when you are with God, as he will keep showing you new things. Old men will dream dreams and still be fruitful in your old age.

Prayerfully ask God to open your eyes of understanding, so you can capture his plan, purpose and mandate for your life; both in the present and in the future. *Jeremiah 33:3. Call unto me, and I will answer thee, and show thee great and mighty things, which thou knowest not.* There are great and mighty things that you do not know now, but God wants to reveal them to you by his Spirit. They are the things that are not obvious to the physical eyes. *1 Corinthians 2:9-11*. God has remarkable things in store for you. However, you must capture them, so you can pursue their fulfilment. Pray against spiritual blindness and stay in God's word to behold your inheritance. *Psalms 119:18. Open my eyes that I may see wonderful things in your law.*

Day 6: *Victorious thought for the day.* Your vision is your future. It is the future that you see that you will ultimately embrace.

PRAYERS.

Father, open my eyes of understanding so I can behold and embrace your wondrous, wonderful and prosperous plans for my life.

Father, I pray that you will grant unto me the spirit of wisdom and revelation in your knowledge, for the pursuit of the destiny you have assigned for me. *Ephesians 1:17*

My father, my father, I pray that you will make known to me whatever I need to know that I am yet to know, in the name of Jesus.

Day 7

I AM FREE INDEED

DAY 7
I AM FREE INDEED

John 8:36. If the Son therefore shall make you free, ye shall be free indeed.

Welcome to another day in this spiritual adventure. It is the day to maximize your inheritance of liberty in Christ. It is your day to experience absolute deliverance from every form of bondage or oppression, so you can experience divine health. When God speaks, no one can stand against it. Jesus has finalized your liberty and deliverance, and no one can annul that.

Luke 13:12-16, Luke 8:35. Matthew 17:15, 17.

SPIRITUAL FACTS.

1. Deliverance and healing are interconnected. Just in the same manner that spiritual bondages and sickness are interconnected. Most of the times, sickness and disease are as a result of demonic oppression, bondages and manipulations. Most of the time, people are sick because of bondages that must be broken. Luke 13:10-12. Mark 5:1-20. Mark 9:25-27. *When Jesus saw that the people came running together, he rebuked the foul spirit, saying unto him, Thou dumb and deaf spirit, I charge thee, come out of him, and enter no more into him.* ²⁶ *And the spirit cried, and rented him sore, and came*

out of him: and he was as one dead; insomuch that many said, He is dead. ²⁷ But Jesus took him by the hand, and lifted him up; and he arose.

2. No matter the state of oppression and sickness, Jesus rules and reigns over them. Jesus raised three dead people in the bible. The daughter of Jairus in *Mark 5* who just died; the son of the woman of Nain in *Luke 7* who already died and whose body was on the way to the cemetery; and in *John 11*, Lazarus already stinking in the grave. The lessons from the three incidences are: Either the problem just started, or has progressed too long (dead on the way to the grave) or already stinking in the grave. These were all obviously beyond any human solution. However, when brought to Jesus, there is absolute hope of healing and restoration.

3. Bondages and spiritual oppression are not to be tolerated but must be rebuked and dealt with. *Matthew 8:16, 17 [AMP]. When evening came, they brought to Him many who were under the power of demons, and He drove out the spirits with a word and restored to health all who were sick. And thus He fulfilled what was spoken by the prophet Isaiah, He Himself took [in order to carry away] our weaknesses and infirmities and bore away our diseases.* So, today is the day to rebuke and drive out all demonic spirits responsible for any affliction or sickness in your body.

WHY?

The battles of life are not physical but invisible battles. We wrestle not against flesh and blood but against principalities. *Ephesians 6:12*. Though we walk in the flesh, our contentions are not in the flesh. *2 Corinthians 10:3-4*. Many people today including Christians have become casualties to damages by Satan, because they are ignorant of this simple spiritual truth. They live their lives with the understanding of the physical world only. What is responsible for the events of life is more than what the physical eyes see. In life, there are forces at war with the intention to derail, enslave, and oppress people. However, just as the devil has his own evil emissaries, God also has his own legions and battalions of hosts of heaven, fighting for his own children. A young man living in Italy was in the bathroom one day preparing to go to work. He heard his name mentioned and answered. The moment he answered, he felt faint and fell down, and became paralyzed. His friend connected him with us, and deliverance was conducted over the phone which led to his total liberation.

HOW DO YOU EXPERIENCE DELIVERANCE?

The spirit world carries out its agenda by erecting altars. Altars are either godly (positive) or satanic (negative) places of operations. An altar is a place where covenants are made with spiritual powers. It is also a place of deliberation, decision, and action, whether negative or positive. Demonic agendas are serviced through demonic altars and godly agendas are serviced on the altar of the cross of Calvary.

Numbers 23.1. And Balaam said unto Balak, Build me here seven altars, and prepare me here seven oxen and seven rams. The devil has counterfeited most things God has instituted to bless His people. The problems of many people can be directly linked to evil altars. The enemies go about to construct altars of affliction for many people and these altars have priests of wickedness ministering on them. The devil has taught his people the secret of altars and they use it for destructive purposes.

The cross where Jesus died was an altar of sacrifice of the Son of God. That cross, therefore, stood for a positive altar, which is meant for good purposes. Conversely, negative altars are raised by the enemies to steal, kill, and destroy.

In *1 Samuel 7:10,* Samuel raised an altar in the name of God against the Philistines, and as a result, God became angry with the Philistines and thundered greatly against them, from heaven. The altar made things easy for the Israelites. God fought for them and they did not have to do anything by themselves. In the spirit world, it is the stronger one that prevails in any conflict. The altar of the cross of Jesus Christ is stronger and more potent than any altar. *Luke 11:21-22.*

Therefore, no matter what evil altar has been raised against your life, you can break loose and be victorious by lifting up the cross of Calvary today. The snake of Moses swallowed that of Egyptian magicians in the court of Pharaoh. The altar of God is superior to that of the devil. The cross of Jesus is the altar of God. Altar of prayers are made in the name of Jesus. When an altar fights an altar the stronger one will prevail. In Egypt, Moses defeated all the gods of Pharaoh. *Exodus 7:12.* Declare forcefully that whatever agents of darkness troubling your destiny are silenced forever in Jesus name.

If we must overcome the altar raised against us, we need another altar. If they are using the names of their gods against us, we are to use the name of our own God; who is Jesus Christ. Use the power in the name of Jesus to liberate yourself from every form of bondage and captivity. *Philippians 2:5-10*

To be free, we also need to walk in the knowledge of your position in Christ. You have been redeemed and repositioned into the heavenly places by Christ Jesus. *Ephesians 2:1-5.* You have been raised up to sit with Christ, far above principalities and powers.

You must know and declare that you cannot be bound or oppressed:

- Because of the superior sacrifice of Jesus Christ on the cross

- Because of the superior altar of the cross of calvary
- Because of the superior covenant through the blood of Jesus Christ. *Hebrews 8:6*
- Because of the superior name of the risen Jesus Christ. *Philippians 2:5-10*
- Because of the superior ordinances and commandments of the word of the lord. *Lamentations 3:37*

Day 7: *Victorious thought for the day.* The stronger one has set me free, therefore no force or power is strong enough to keep me in bondage. I am free indeed.

PRAYERS

By the power in the blood of Jesus, I liberate my destiny from any form of bondage to self, sin, and Satan.

I decree that this is my day of total liberation from any bondage and oppression. This is my day of total restoration of my original purpose and destiny.

Every shackle, fetter of darkness holding me in bondage, I command you to break now and forever, in the name of Jesus.

Day 8

ARISE AND BE HEALED

DAY 8
ARISE AND BE HEALED

Mark 2:11, 12 [NKJV]. I say to you, arise, take up your bed, and go to your house. Immediately he arose, took up the bed, and went out in the presence of them all, so that all were amazed and glorified God, saying, "We never saw anything like this!"

This is the set day and time to arise and embrace your covenant of healing. I am convinced in my spirit that this is your hour to embrace the dimensions of healing you have never enjoyed. The word "immediately" in the scriptures above was very scarce in the Old Testament; it however occurred 59 times in the New Testament in regards to healing. Simply because the day Jesus announced on the cross that *"it is finished,"* your warfare and mine were over. That was the day that Jesus established our dominion over Satan; dominion over his operations in our lives which include sicknesses and diseases. It was that day that your healing package was secured and delivered. *1 Peter 2:24 [NKJV]. Who Himself bore our sins in His own body on the tree, that we, having died to sins, might live for righteousness – by whose stripes you were healed.*

In *Matthew 13*, when he encountered Jesus, the man that was full of leprosy received immediate cleansing. When he met Jesus Christ, the man in *Mark 2* rose up immediately. The woman of the issue of blood also experienced instantaneous miracle when she encountered Jesus Christ. Jesus remains the same and has not changed. Hebrews 13:8. This is your day to experience immediate healing and restoration in your health.

We also saw the power of instant healing like Jesus', in the ministry of the disciples. *Acts 3:16.* Peter's shadow healed people. *Acts 5:15-16. Insomuch that they brought forth the sick into the streets, and laid them on beds and couches, that at least the shadow of Peter passing by might overshadow some of them. There came also a multitude out of the cities roundabout unto Jerusalem, bringing sick folks, and them which were vexed with unclean spirits: and they were healed everyone.*

Acts 14:8-10. And there sat a certain man at Lystra, impotent in his feet, being a cripple from his mother's womb, who never had walked: The same heard Paul speak: who steadfastly beholding him, and perceiving that he had faith to be healed, Said with a loud voice, Stand upright on thy feet. And he leaped and walked.

Every record of instant healing in the scripture is a product of definite and desperate moves. No one got it sitting and waiting. You confront it and go after it at every cost. Everyone that benefited from it made definite and desperate moves. Matthew 11:12. The woman of issue of blood took steps in her weakness and got the breakthrough.

FACTORS THAT GENERATE IMMEDIATE HEALING

1. First, recognize that your total health package has been fully paid for. This type of understanding becomes the fuel to provoke your desperation for healing. *1 Corinthians 6:20. For ye are bought with a price: therefore glorify God in your body, and in your spirit, which are God's.*
2. Healing is the legal and moral right of every child of God. *Matthew 15:26.* We are god's priority on this earth for health and vitality. Every child of God is ordained to live a super healthy life.

3. Recognize also that your warfare against sickness was accomplished on the cross. *John 19:30. Isaiah 41*
4. Recognize that every sickness is an oppression of the devil, but at redemption, you were redeemed from oppression. *Acts 10:38. Isaiah 54:14, 15 [NKJV]. In righteousness you shall be established; you shall be far from oppression, for you shall not fear; And from terror, for it shall not come near you. Indeed they shall surely assemble, but not because of Me. whoever assembles against you shall fall for your sake.*

   Redemption removes you and I far from oppression. You are no longer a candidate for demonic oppression. Satanic oppression became illegal by redemption. *Colossians 1:13. Who hath delivered us from the power of darkness, and hath translated us into the kingdom of his dear Son.* Every believer has been removed from the oppression of darkness. This revelation becomes the bedrock for your authority and conviction. If my redemption is real and I know that it is, then I can no longer be held in bondage. Therefore, the wickedness of the devil can never be expressed in my life. Your redemption changes your position spiritually. You have been removed from where Satan operates to where he cannot operate. So you do not wait for miracles, you work out your miracles. Blind Bartimaeus knew that it was his day; he cried out for a touch. This is the beginning of the season for your to forcefully take your healing and deliverance from sickness and disease You do not just wish for it, you go after it, beginning with an inner holy indignation.
5. Look at your body in the eyes of Jesus and take your liberty by force. *Hebrews 12:1-3. John 20:21. As the father has sent me so sent I thee.* Since God sent you in the same capacity like Jesus, whatever cannot afflict Jesus, cannot afflict you. So you can and must ask the question; "Would this sickness have survived on Jesus?" Tell yourself that it will

amount to abuse of redemption for me to accommodate and tolerate sickness.

One of the greatest obstacles for your healing and deliverance is doubt and unbelief. Have faith in the faithfulness of God to fulfil his words. Have faith in the power of the blood of Jesus shed for your healing. Have faith in the word of God being able to build you up and give you your healing inheritance. *Acts 20:32.*

Avoid murmuring and complaining; it opens the door to the destroyer. You will never leave a healthy life when you murmur. God is not the one responsible for the challenges of your life; he is your helper. *1 Corinthians 10:10. Neither murmur ye, as some of them also murmured, and were destroyed of the destroyer.*

As such, today, identify your enemy - his name is the devil.

Identify your healer, his name is Jehovah Rapha.

Identify your physicians, his name is Jesus Christ, the son of God.

Identify the balm that heals of sicknesses and diseases; it is the word of God.

You need to declare boldly the following:

I have been translated, so I can no longer be afflicted. I have been translated, so I can no longer be tormented. I have been translated, so my case is settled. I have been translated, so the price has been paid. Arise and be healed, the price has been paid.

WHY SHOULD I DECLARE HEALING?

Jesus took them on the cross. *Matthew 8:17. That it might be fulfilled which was spoken by Esaias the prophet, saying, Himself took our infirmities, and bare our sicknesses. Psalms 18:44-45. As soon as they hear of me, they shall obey me: the strangers shall submit themselves unto me. The strangers shall fade away, and be afraid out of their close places.*

Whatever is foreign to your body and to your destiny is a stranger. They must hear you, obey you, submit themselves to you and fade away. Sicknesses, diseases, oppression, poverty and sin are strangers that must fade away from your body

Day 8: *Victorious thought for the day*. The price for my wellness, wholeness and divine health has been paid, therefore I cannot be sick and will not be sick.

PRAYERS

In the name of Jesus, I cast all infirmities and sickness on the cross of Calvary

Every poison in my body, physical, biological, chemical and spiritual, be flushed out by the blood of Jesus now.

Every evil presence at night, be cast out and destroyed in Jesus name.

Every strange noise in the head, be removed in Jesus name.

Every strange feeling in the heart; every palpitation in the heart, be shaken out now.

Every pain of mobility, moving from one point of the body to the other, I receive healing by the stripes of Jesus Christ.

I declare wholeness, wellness and healing, from the top of my head to the soles of my feet, in the name of Jesus.

In the name of Jesus, I reject a life of sickness and disease, and I embrace divine health.

Day 9

HOW TO SECURE DIVINE HELP

DAY 9
HOW TO SECURE DIVINE HELP

This is your day and season to place a demand on God and the breakthrough anointing for divine intervention. I have a burden and a witness in my heart for you to pray and see a turnaround especially on long standing issues. This is your season to press for divine intervention in regards to every issue bothering you.

This world is a battlefield and without divine help, you will suffer defeat, humiliation, and shame. Without divine help, people will forget you and men will abandon you. Help is assistance given to somebody in order to make things easier, better, or possible. Where there is difficulty, you need help.

The help of God is the answer to all helplessness in life. Career helplessness. Medical helplessness. Financial helplessness. I need you to magnify the help of God, situation irrespective, because the help of God can resolve all issues.

God has revealed himself in his word as the helper. God has promised to give all the help we will ever need in life. *Psalms 10:14. Thou hast seen it; for thou beholdest mischief and spite, to requite it with thy hand: the poor committeth himself unto thee; thou art the helper of the fatherless.* When you see us chasing after God madly, it is because our God is too faithful to fail us. *Psalms 72:12. For he* *shall deliver the needy when he crieth; the poor also, and him that hath no helper.*

Anyone helped by God cannot remain helpless in life. This year God will deliver you from suffering. This is the season to cry out for the help of the Lord.

THINGS TO KNOW ABOUT HELP FROM ABOVE

Help comes from above and not from abroad. There are many people looking at the wrong direction for help. The help you need is not from abroad. The help that will sustain you is from above. When you connect to God above, he will connect you with man. **Heaven controls the earth.** If you touch the heaven, heaven will touch you. God's hands are so long and can touch everywhere. If God connects you no one can disconnect you. *James 1:17. Psalms 46:1. God is our refuge and strength, a very present help in trouble.* That means a helper that does not fail. A help that is present when you need it, how you need and where you need it. Psalms 121:2. No matter what is confronting you in life, always look up and never look down. When you look down, you magnify your problem. If you can look up, you will get up. When you look down, you lose things. When you look up you gain things. God is our all-sufficient and ultimate helper. *Hebrews 4:16.*

Every human being is limited and requires help. There is no self-sufficient man. The rich need help. The poor need help. The young need help. The old need help. In fact, the higher you go the more help you need. They that are on the floor do not fear falling.

Psalms 72:12. For he will deliver the needy when he cries for help, The afflicted also, and him who has no helper.

He is the helper of the poor, needy, and the helpless. He will deliver them when they cry for help. There is no help we need that God cannot provide. *Genesis 2:18*. Even if what you need is not available, God can provide custom-made help.

Rest assured, the help of God always comes on time. Timely provisions and supplies, on time. Marriage, on time. School fees, on time. House mortgage, on time. It might not come when you think, but the help of God will always come on time. He is our very present help. *Psalms 46:5. God is in the midst of her; she shall not be moved: God shall help her, and that right early.* If you expect God to manifest on time, he will be on time, if you pray with a resurrection day mindset. *Ezekiel 12*.

When you recognize God as your help, He will mobilize all other channels for your help. Whoever is connected to your blessing, they are under pressure to release it.

WHEN IS IT NECESSARY TO SECURE THE HELP OF GOD?

It is necessary in situations where you have done all that you can, without any desired result. In *Luke 5*, Apostle Peter went fishing at the right time, with the right tools, right skills, and with the right team, but yet, caught nothing. He became discouraged and gave up, until Jesus stepped in and gave him a miraculous fish-catching experience. God steps in on occasions when it is beyond the ability of man to help.

2 Kings 6:26-27. Then, as the king of Israel was passing by on the wall, a woman cried out to him, saying, "Help, my lord, O king! And he said, "If the LORD does not help you, where can I find help for you? There was a terrible drought in the land; so bad that women resulted into eating their children. Some women cried out to the king for help and he replied, that if God would not help, no one could.

It is necessary when no one is willing to help, or when those who want to help may fail. *John 5:1-9*. My wife and I got a distress call from a lady in 2008, regarding her husband's situation. The husband was in a teaching hospital as a Resident. It was discovered that he had an infection in his blood that needed treatment, to avoid infecting his patients and others. He was given the option of either taking medication for curing the condition or to withdraw from the program. The condition became worse from the complications that arose from the medications. The man could not function in the classroom; he was in the hospital and was just flat out mentally distressed. To the glory of God, after series of prayers, he regained his sanity and strength to complete his residency and is now a practicing medical doctor.

It is necessary when there are altars of darkness erected against your progress.

It is necessary because God never intended for us to face life's troubles by ourselves. *John 16:33*. God knows that we are in a hostile territory governed by Satan, the god of this world. God promised us help. He does not hold back help from his people. God has documented his promise to help us, in his word. As a loving and caring father, he is available to help us in the time of our needs.

Psalms 46:1-5 [NLT]. God is our refuge and strength, always ready to help in times of trouble. So we will not fear when earthquakes come and the mountains crumble into the sea. Let the oceans roar and foam. Let the mountains tremble as the waters surge! A river brings joy to the city of our God, the sacred home of the Most High. God dwells in that city; it cannot be destroyed. From the very break of day, God will protect it.

He is willing, able, and available to help. He never slumbers nor sleeps.

One of the differences between a Christian and a non-Christian is that no matter what we are faced with, it is never hopeless. Irrespective of where you are or whatever is happening in your life, you are always a candidate for divine intervention. *Job 14:7-9*.

HOW DO YOU SECURE DIVINE HELP?

Through persistent prayer. *Psalms 50:15: and call upon me in the day of trouble: I will deliver thee, and thou shall glorify me.* Prayer is the avenue for getting God involved in your battles. There can never be the release of heavens' blessings on the earth without an earthly initiation. Your prayer is the earthly invitation for heavenly invasion of your destiny. Prayer creates a shift in the spirit realm that impacts the physical. When king Herod rose against the church in *Acts 12*, the church prayed without ceasing. God responded in heaven, broke the chains of Apostle Peter and released him from jail. The power of God dealt with king Herod by eliminating him, and the work of God grew.

When you commit God to his word. Abraham got God involved in saving Sodom and Gomorrah by committing him to his word. *Genesis 18:23. Psalms 89:134. I will say of the Lord, He is my Refuge and my Fortress, my God; on Him I lean and rely, and in Him I [confidently] trust!*

When you declare his word. When challenges and obstacles arise, declare that God is your refuge and strength. When you wake up with an attitude of faith and expectancy and declare God's Word, you will be strengthened and empowered by His Spirit. *Joel 3:10. Let the weak say, "I am strong."* Let the single say, "I am married," etc.

Isaiah 3:10. Say to the righteous, that it shall be well with him for they shall eat the fruit of their doings.

Through sacrificial faith-giving to God or to his prophets, you can provoke divine help. Whenever you sow into kingdom agenda and into the life or the ministry of a man of God, you are provoking the anointing placed upon him or her. The testimony of scripture is that when people needed the move of God they laid things on the altar. The woman with the alabaster jar. *Matthew 26:7*. Tabitha-Dorcas in *Acts 9:36-41*. Her sacrificial seed spoke for her, even when she was already dead.

Day 9: *Victorious thought for the day*. The help of God is the answer to all helplessness in life. Anyone helped by God cannot remain helpless in life.

PRAYERS

Revelation 12:13-16. Father, I pray today that all the elements of the earth will begin to help me, and nothing is permitted to hurt my destiny.

Oh earth, oh earth, I command you by the word of the Lord, help me to succeed, help me to breakthrough, and help my family to succeed, in the name of Jesus

My father, my father, let your favor connect me with destiny helpers who will use their resources to help me in Jesus name.

Day 10

WISDOM - YOUR POWER INTO THE WORLD OF UNLIMITED MANIFESTATIONS

DAY 10
WISDOM - YOUR POWER INTO THE WORLD OF UNLIMITED MANIFESTATIONS

Proverbs 8:15. By me kings reign, and princes decree justice.

Welcome to your day of wisdom manifestations. In the school of manifestations of destiny, wisdom is a must. One of the vital covenant requirements for a life of unlimited manifestations is divine wisdom. *Proverbs 8:15-16.*

Wisdom is a key that unlocks the door to the world of unlimited exploits and unlimited manifestations. What anointing gathers, wisdom preserves, but what anointing gathers, foolishness can also scatter. The difference between the haves and the have-nots is sometimes wisdom. God's dream is to make you a blessing just as he made Abraham great. *Psalms 51:2.* Look unto your father Abraham, and desire to flow in the wisdom of God.

FOUR TYPES OF WISDOM

James 3:15-17, James 1:5.

- Earthly wisdom - known as common sense.
- Sensual and intellectual wisdom – from rigorous engagement in the process of learning.

- Devilish or diabolical wisdom - through manipulation of men,
- Heavenly wisdom - from above.

Wisdom from above is simply operating by divine instructions. *Matthew 7:24-27. Psalms 119:105.* Examples in the bible include:

Joseph who by wisdom ruled and reigned in every situation he found himself. While in Potiphar's house as a slave, he reigned by wisdom. While in the prison, he reigned by wisdom, and ultimately it was wisdom that lifted him to the position of a prime minister in Egypt. *Genesis 41:38-39*

You do not elect a wise man; wisdom selects him. Wisdom causes you to be needed.

Daniel operated for a period of 65 years under six different kings. *Daniel 1:17-20.*

When a man is empowered by wisdom, his reign continues. *Daniel 6:1-3. Solomon 1. Kings 3:15. 1 Kings 4:29.*

Paul the apostle was almost a picture of misfortune. When Christ was alive, he was around but did not follow him. When the church began, he became an enemy of the church. However, by wisdom, he became the first of all the Apostles.

2 Peter 3:15. And consider that the longsuffering of our Lord is salvation — as also our beloved brother Paul, according to the wisdom given to him, has written to you, [16] as also in all his epistles, speaking in them of these things, in which are some things hard to understand, which untaught and unstable people twist to their own destruction, as they do also the rest of the Scriptures.

By wisdom, Apostle Paul was used of God for massive exploits and God desires the same for you and me.

HOW DO I ENGAGE OR TAP INTO THE WISDOM OF GOD FOR UNLIMITED MANIFESTATIONS?

1. Engage the altar of prayer by faith. *James 1:5-8*. Wisdom is available to those who ask in faith. God will not refuse the man who asks him in faith. *Jeremiah 33:3. 1 Kings 3:3, 13*. Solomon got it through prayer. Make sure you pray daily that God should baptize you with his divine wisdom for profitable living.
2. Be committed to searching and meditating on scriptures. *2 Timothy 3:15*. When you take in God's word, you become wise. *Psalms 1:2-3. Psalms 119:97-100*.
3. Engage the help of the Holy Spirit. *Isaiah 11:2-3*. There are seven dimensions of his operations. The Holy Spirit is also referred to as the spirit of wisdom. *Ephesians 1:17*.
4. Engage the ministry of your God-ordained teachers. *Isaiah 30:20-21. 2 Chronicles 26:5*.
5. Confront situations with the consciousness of the mind of Christ at work in you. *1 Corinthians 2:16*. That means, no matter the situation you are in, there is a way out.

Day 10: *Victorious thought for the day.* Wisdom is the promoter and the preserver of destiny. What grace gives, wisdom preserves, and whatever grace gives; foolishness scatters. So be wise.

PRAYERS

Father, I pray that you will baptize me afresh daily with your wisdom for profitable living.

By the authority in the word of God, I pray that God will make me wise in all things, to know what to do in all situations.

I reject and rebuke foolishness out of my life now and forever.

I declare boldly that I have the wisdom of Jesus flowing and operating through me for profitable living in Jesus name.

Day 11

LIVING A LIFE OF IMPACT

DAY 11
LIVING A LIFE OF IMPACT

Acts 10:38. John 14:12. Matthew 5:13-15, Ephesians 2:8-10

John 18:37 KJV. Pilate therefore said unto him, Art thou a king then? Jesus answered, Thou sayest that I am a king. To this end was I born, and for this cause came I into the world, that I should bear witness unto the truth. Every one that is of the truth hears my voice.

As you press on in this adventure of faith for unlimited manifestations, this is the day to set your mind on living a life of impact.

1. The core of manifestations in the kingdom is impact. To be fruitful, multiple, subdue and have dominion is to live a life of undeniable and unlimited impact. *Genesis 1:28. Then God blessed them, and God said to them, "Be fruitful and multiply; fill the earth and subdue it; have dominion over the fish of the sea, over the birds of the air, and over every living thing that [a]moves on the earth."*

2. Living a life of impact is our mandate. There are two types of people in life - those who leave scars and those who make a positive impact. People who leave scars impart negative impressions. Years after her death, Mother Theresa's legacy lives on in India and around the world. She was never married and never gave birth to her own children; yet, she was a mother to thousands of lepers and

poor children in India. You and I have been called to make good and great impact especially in our families, communities and generations. *Isaiah 58:12 GWT. Your people will rebuild the ancient ruins and restore the foundations of past generations. You will be called the Rebuilder of Broken Walls and the Restorer of Streets Where People Live.* Irrespective of the condition of your birth (place, status, or the person who gave birth to you), you were born to make a difference and a positive impact in your generation. It is very unfortunate that there are certain people who have allowed their backgrounds to discourage them from a life of meaning and substance.

WHAT DOES IT MEAN TO LIVE A LIFE OF IMPACT?

1. It means to add value to your generation.
2. It means to make positive contributions wherever you are.
3. To do something useful and practical in advancing the course of mankind with the aim of promoting the gospel of Jesus Christ.
4. It means being a blessing to others.
5. It means being a solution and a hope giver.
6. It means adding value to whatever resources you are given. The value of life lies not in the length of days, but in the value added to people, places, and things. A man may live long yet live very little. *Acts 13:36. Now when David had served God's purpose in his own generation, he fell asleep; he was buried with his ancestors and his body decayed.*

There are four categories of people in life, and what you are determines what measure of impact you make in life:

1. DIVIDERS - Always reducing the value of things and people. Are you a divider?

2. **MULTIPLIERS** - Always increasing the value of things and people. Are you a multiplier?
3. **ADDERS** - Always putting in "the extra" into the value of things and people. Are you an addition?
4. **SUBTRACTORS** - Always removing from the value of things and people. Are you a subtraction?

Choose daily to live as either an "Adder" or a "Multiplier."

THINGS TO KNOW

1. **YOU WERE BORN ON PURPOSE FOR A PURPOSE.** *John 18:37.* In order to live a life of impact, the first thing to know is that your existence on this earth is not by accident. You must know that you are not an accident, or a mistake and you are definitely not a misfit. You are a creation of intentionality. You may not have been planned by your parents, but you were planned by God, long before you were born. *2 Timothy 1:9 [TLB].* You were not chosen by last minute decision. You were brought here at this moment in order to fulfil a need.

   As Rick Warren said, we were not born just because our parents decided to have children. We are not on the earth simply to exist from day to day. We are here as Christians because God has known us before the universe was made. He called us before the universe began. He has a reason for us to be alive and those who devote their lives to Him will know that reason. *Ephesians 2:20. For we are His workmanship, created in Christ Jesus for good works, which God prepared beforehand that we should walk in them.*

   Satan lies to people that you are just a number. You should understand that no manufacturer produces a material first before he determines the purpose. He must determine the purpose of the very thing, prior to producing it. Similarly, your purpose for existence was determined by God first, before you came to this world. *Jeremiah 1:5. For we are his workmanship, created in Christ Jesus unto good works, which God hath before ordained that we should walk in them.*

2. **YOU WERE BORN TO BE DIFFERENT SO YOU CAN MAKE A DIFFERENCE.** Isaiah 42:6 [NLT]. I, the Lord, have called you to demonstrate my righteousness. I will take you by the hand and guard you, and I will give you my people, Israel, as a symbol of my covenant with them. And you will be a light to guide the nations. I am bringing you out of Egypt for a purpose to be a light to all nations. Jeremiah 1:5. 1 Peter 2:9-12. You were not chosen by God just to fit in; you were chosen by God to stand out. God did not save you to blend in and look just like the rest of the world. Matthew 5:13-16 [MSG].

HOW DO I MAKE IMPACT?

1. Discover your unique gifts. What are your talents. What are the experiences you have that are uniquely different from others? 1 Peter 4:10 KJV. As every man hath received the gift, even so minister the same one to another, as good stewards of the manifold grace of God.
2. Use those gifts and experiences to serve others, especially the interest of God's kingdom. 1 Timothy 4:11.NLV. Be sure to use the gift God gave you. The leaders saw this in you when they laid their hands on you and said what you should do. God did not give you the gifts and talents to serve yourself. We live as part of a self-centered generation. A generation that is wrapped up in self, even in the use of God-given gifts. Maybe you have the gift of being business-minded or the gift of music (singing, playing musical instruments, etc.). You must realize that God uses

your gifts and experiences to heal others. Luke 2. I must be about my father's business. Y

3. You need a vision that is bigger and better than yourself. You need a mission that demands every second of your time, every ounce of your talents, and every penny of your treasure. Then, you will not want to waste it on lesser things. Instead of focusing on what you are not going to do, focus on what you want to do. The best way to overcome your issue is to help someone else who has issues. Live a life dedicated to God's service, especially sacrifices for kingdom advancement. Exodus 23:22 & 25. Job 36:11. Matthew 6:33. Who seeks you is determined by who you seek. What seeks you is determined by what you seek. We do not beg to be blessed in God's kingdom; we serve to be blessed. Exodus 23:25. We serve to be healed. Exodus 23:25. Proverbs 13:29. 2 Corinthians 5:20. Our promotion is based on our faithful stewardship. Luke 19:17. We serve to be honored. John 12:26. Proverbs 14:28. 1 Samuel 2:30. We serve to be fruitful. Exodus 23:26. No more dry season in my life, in the name of Jesus.

4. By sharing our faith. You do not have to be saved for more than a minute for you to be qualified to share your faith. A blind man did, in John 9. You do not need theological training to be able to share the gospel. Matthew 28:18-20.

CHARACTERISTICS OF THOSE LIVING TO MAKE IMPACT

1. You must be vision and kingdom driven. Every great leader who imparted his or her generation had a vision for it. They were vision and purpose driven. Without vision you can achieve nothing. *Proverbs 29:18*. Jesus had a vision to save humanity from sin and its consequences. Nelson

Mandela had a vision to liberate South Africa from colonial oppression and suppression. Martin Luther king had a vision to see an America that was free from all forms of racial segregation. The Wright brothers had a vision to make a machine which could fly like a bird.

2. Exceptional character. *Matthew 7:16*. Men and women who have made a difference possess an exceptional character. You cannot make a positive impact with a questionable character. It is said that qualifications, skills, giftings and hard work can help you to rise to places of prominence, but it takes exceptional character to remain there. *Psalms 78:72. And David shepherded them with integrity of heart; with skillful hands he led them.*

3. They are sacrifice oriented. If at all you want to make a difference, self-sacrifice is a must. Great leaders are produced at the altar of sacrifice. Making a difference and making impact must cost you something. You must be willing to deny yourself of certain things for the sake of the greater cause. It cost Jesus his life. Nelson Mandela sacrificed and gave all and refused to come out of prison until the South Africans were liberated from colonial oppression.

4. Faith. It takes faith and absolute trust in the word of God in order to positively affect your world. *Hebrews 11:33. Men who through faith subdued kingdoms, wrought righteousness, obtained promises, stopped the mouths of lions.*

5. Courage and boldness. World changers do not bow down to fear and opposing forces. Courage and boldness distinguishes them from the rest. Fearful and timid people achieve nothing. *Proverbs 28:1. The wicked flee though no one pursues, but the righteous are as bold as a lion.* Your boldness comes as a result of your trust in the living God and His abilities. IF I PERISH; I PERISH, said Esther in *Esther 4:16. Go, gather together all the Jews that are present in Shushan, and*

> *fast ye for me, and neither eat nor drink three days, night or day: I and my maidens will fast likewise; and so will I go in unto the king, which is not according to the law: and if I perish, I perish.*

Day 11: *Victorious thought for the day.* The mark of a person is not in what you consume but the lives you affect positively.

PRAYERS

Father, I embrace grace to be a problem solver in my generation and beyond in Jesus name.

From now and henceforth; I receive the grace not to live for self, but rather to live a life of impact, and to be a blessing to my family, the church of God and my generation, in Jesus name.

I reject a life of barrenness and embrace a life of fruitfulness.

I receive the grace to be a destiny helper to those who cross my path in this life.

Day 12

ENGAGING THE VOICE OF GOD FOR UNLIMITED MANIFESTATIONS

DAY 12
ENGAGING THE VOICE OF GOD FOR UNLIMITED MANIFESTATIONS

The value of a man/woman does not consist of the valuables he/she possesses. *Luke 2:15. And He said to them, Take heed and beware of covetousness, for one's life does not consist in the abundance of the things he possesses. Matthew 20:26. Yet it shall not be so among you; but whoever desires to become great among you, let him be your servant.* The value and the greatness of a man in this kingdom is the impact s/he makes.

One of the foundational factors for making impact is having access to the voice of God. As we journey further into this adventure, we are going to maximize our faith in hearing the voice of God. Nobody makes impact in this kingdom without an access into the voice of God. You can only speak for God whom you have heard from. The exploits and impact made by Jesus was predicated on his ability to hear from God. *John 15:19. Jesus gave them this answer: Very truly I tell you, the Son can do nothing by himself; he can do only what he sees his Father doing, because whatever the Father does the Son also does.*

It was obedience to the voice of God that Abraham made a generational impact. *Genesis 12:1-4.* At each step of elevation or manifestation for Abraham, it was as a result of response to God's direction. When God is your guide, supernatural breakthroughs become your experience. *Psalms 23:1, 6*. The voice of God is the GPS in this wild world, which has the devil on the loose, with a mission to steal, kill and destroy. *John 10:4, 27*. Do you desire a life of impact and meaning today, set your mind to hear from God.

WHY DO I NEED ACCESS TO THE VOICE OF GOD?

1. We are a generation that is surrounded by many voices speaking to us. Some of the voices can bring confusion, fear, and intimidation, but God's voice will always guarantee victory. *1 Corinthians 14:10. There are, it may be, so many kinds of voices in the world, and none of them is without signification.*
2. Access to the voice of God is a proof of your sonship. One of the proofs that you are a child is the ability to recognize the voice of your heavenly father and follow given instructions. *John 10:27. My sheep hear My voice, and I know them, and they follow Me.* Access to the voice of God is our birthright in redemption. It is not for some special people. It is just a natural occurrence. You do not have to go to school to know the voice of your mother and father. Every child of God has automatic access to the voice of God, if you know how to tune in. *Romans 8:14. For as many as are led by the Spirit of God, these are the sons of God. Conversely, this scripture implies that if we are God's children, if we are born-again, we will be led by His Spirit.*
3. Access to the voice of God helps you in making accurate decisions, avoiding the trap of living by trial and error. Life is a series of decision-making processes. *Proverbs 14:12. There is a way that appears to be right, but in the end it leads to death. Isaiah 48:17.*
4. You are able to enjoy the blessings of proper location and allocation. *Psalms 23:2-3.*

No matter how you train your pet, can they speak your language? Your pet cannot give you a summary of the news on TV. Nothing you do can make your pet speak the language of humans. You have to be human to hear the voice of humans. Likewise, you have to be of the spirit to hear the voice of the spirit. No matter how "churchy" you are, if you are not a person of the spirit, you cannot capture God's voice. Hence, only those who have the spirit of God can access the voice of God. *Romans 8:6 [NIV]. The mind governed by the flesh is death, but the mind governed by the Spirit is life and peace [NLT]. So letting your sinful nature control your mind leads to death. But letting the Spirit control your mind leads to life and peace.*

Revelation 1:10. I was in the Spirit on the Lord's Day, and I heard behind me a loud voice, as of a trumpet [NLT]. It was the Lord's Day, and I was worshiping in the Spirit. Suddenly, I heard behind me a loud voice like a trumpet blast. Revelation 2:7. He who has an ear, let him hear what the Spirit says to the churches.

HOW DO I ENGAGE THE VOICE OF GOD?

To access the voice of God, you must desire to be spiritual. You must connect daily with the person of the Holy Spirit. He is the connecting line between you and God. *John 4:24 says, God is a Spirit: and they that worship him must worship him in spirit and in truth. 1 Corinthians 2:9-12.*

Communication with God is Spirit to spirit, not brain to brain, or mouth to ear. God speaks to our spirits, in thoughts and impressions and not in words. People state; "I think the Lord wants me to do this or that." "I think I should do . . ." Therefore, we often miss the leading of the Lord, thinking it is our own thoughts. When it comes to direction, many are seeking the spectacular and missing the supernatural. *1 Kings 19:12. ..and after the earthquake a fire, but the Lord was not in the fire; and after the fire, a still small voice.* How? Inward witness. Through God's spirit with our spirit.

(Sometimes you can't explain it, but you just know it). *Romans 8:14, 16. For as many as are led by the Spirit of God, they are the sons of God. For ye have not received the spirit of bondage again to fear; but ye have received the Spirit of adoption, whereby we cry, Abba, Father. The Spirit itself bears witness with our spirit, that we are the children of God:*

We need to become spirit conscious. Spiritual things will be elusive to us until we become spirit conscious. The more spiritually conscious we become, the more real the leadings of the Lord. *1 Thessalonians 5:23. And the very God of peace sanctify you wholly; and I pray God your whole spirit and soul and body be preserved blameless unto the coming of our Lord Jesus Christ.*

1. With our spirit we contact the spiritual world.
2. With our soul we contact the mental world.
3. With our body using the five senses we contact the physical world.

Feeling is the voice of the body; reasoning is the voice of the mind; and conscience, intuition, or the inner voice is the voice of the spirit. *1 Timothy 4:2*

HOW DO I HEAR FROM GOD?

Habakkuk said, *I will stand on my guard post..." Hab. 2:1. Psalm 46:10. Be still, and know that I am God. Psalm 37:7 [NLT]. Be still in the presence of the Lord, and wait patiently for him to act. Don't worry about evil people who prosper or fret about their wicked schemes. Mark 1:35-40.*

1. **Take time out to seek God's face and wait to hear from him.** The first key to hearing God's voice is to avoid distraction. Learn to practice quietness and stillness. Avoid a life of busyness. It is in the stillness, not busyness, that we tune our spiritual ears to hear the voice of God. The Lord always speaks to us in that "STILL, small voice" (*1 Kings*

19:12, emphasis mine), but often it is drowned out amid all the turmoil of our daily lives. *Luke 6:12-13*. God may not speak immediately but he will surely speak. Continue to be conscious and eager to hear from him on any particular issue.

At the start of our church in 1999, my wife and I wanted a location in Queens, New York. This was to create a significant physical distance between the location of our former church and our new ministry. We kept praying for divine direction as we began to search for a building in Queens. One Monday morning while my wife and me were driving around in search of a building, I heard the voice of the Holy Spirit on North Conduit Avenue at Guy R. Boulevard. God said, "Who is sending you to Queens?" Right there and then, we stopped driving and thanked God for the answer to our quest. We thank God for his direction, because our divinely orchestrated choice of location significantly contributed to the impressive start of the church.

2. **Be committed to a life of prayer and fasting.** Fasting and prayer will clear off all the distractions and clogs in your spiritual ears. *Isaiah 58:11*. Fasting is prescribed for accessing divine guidance. *Isaiah 58:6*. It empowers access to the voice of God. *Matthew 6:16*.

Whenever God speaks to you, it can be confirmed by:

1. His word. God's will can never contradict his word. God will never tell you to violate what he already gave in his word. *Luke 21:33*. Opinion changes, science changes, but truth never changes. *Psalms 119:105*. Your word is a lamp for my feet, a light on my path. *Hebrews 4:12*. Your faith must be based on the word of God and not your feelings.

2. **The peace of God inside of your soul.** When God speaks to you, peace is the umpire for confirmation. There is peace and rest in every area of your life, when God has spoken. Peace is the evidence that God has spoken. Let the peace of God be a filter. Peace is the judge and jury. Anything you are not at peace with, do not do it. *Colossians 3:15 [AMP]. And let the peace (soul harmony which comes) from Christ rule (act as umpire continually) in your hearts [deciding and settling with finality all questions that arise in your minds, in that peaceful state] to which as [members of Christ's] one body you were also called [to live]. And be thankful (appreciative), [giving praise to God always]."* How do you know when it is the peace of God? When it passes all other understanding. *Philippians 4:7.* When you do not have a resolution to the issue at hand, yet you have the utmost peace.
3. **By the mouth of two or three witnesses.** *By the mouth of two or three witnesses every fact may be confirmed. Matthew 18:16.* There can be confirmation through spirit filled people.
4. *Through* anointed counsel. There are certain things you will not know except by divine counsel through your shepherd. The day you no longer hear from your man or woman of God, you stop hearing from God at a greater dimension. *Jeremiah 3:15. And I will give you pastors according to mine heart, which shall feed you with knowledge and understanding.* Archbishop Idahosa heard from his pastor this scripture. *Matthew10:7-8. And as ye go, preach, saying, The kingdom of heaven is at hand. Heal the sick, cleanse the lepers, raise the dead, cast out devils: freely ye have received, freely give.* The day you see your pastor as mere man or become too familiar, you stop hearing a dimension of God.

Seek and ask God today to speak to you on those specific issues of your life and trust him by faith to do so. Begin to attune your spiritual ears to his direction, into your spirit man. Whatever you hear him say, step out in obedience. You are about to step into a new dimension, and nothing can stop your shining forth. This is because when God sends you, He backs you up with his resources.

Day 12: *Victorious thought for the day.* When God speaks over your life, all confusion ceases.

PRAYERS

Father, I receive healing from every spiritual deafness in Jesus name.

By the authority in the name of Jesus, I will not be confused in the journey of life.

My father, my father, make known to me your plans and purpose for this season.

I receive the spirit of obedience to follow divine instructions completely, in Jesus name.

I receive the grace and strength to obey divine instructions, in Jesus name.

From today and henceforth, I will be at the right place at the right time obtaining the right results, in Jesus name.

Day 13

I AM AUTHORIZED FOR FINANCIAL ABUNDANCE

DAY 13
I AM AUTHORIZED FOR FINANCIAL ABUNDANCE

Welcome to this special day of financial abundance and financial favor. There is an all-sufficient financial grace that will be released upon your life as you prayerfully meditate on this material. Financial abundance is your heritage in redemption. Money is a tool of unlimited manifestations. *Ecclesiastes 10:19. A feast is made for laughter, and wine makes merry: but money answers all things.*

God wants you to have it so you can reign as kings. Zechariah 1:17. *Deuteronomy 28:12. The Lord shall open unto thee his good treasure, the heaven to give the rain unto thy land in his season, and to bless all the work of thine hand: and thou shalt lend unto many nations, and thou shalt not borrow.*

God wants you to have financial abundance so you can become a blessing to others. *Genesis 12:1-3*. He wants you to be a conduit of blessing to your family, the church of God, and to your generation. *2 Corinthians 9:8 [CEV]*. He wants you to be able to finance the cause of Christ's mission on the earth. The gospel is free but the means to convey it is not free. Money enhances the vocal power of the church. One of the vehicles for promoting the kingdom of God on the earth is the generosity of God's people. And you cannot support the kingdom work financially, when you are in lack. *Luke 7:5.*

Salvation is also an all rounded encounter. Salvation does not only deliver from sin, but also from financial struggles. It is a total package of deliverance, preservation, protection and prosperity in every area of our lives. By redemptive covenant, God does not want you to have financial pressure; he wants you to have financial power. *Job 36:11. If they obey and serve him, they shall spend their days in prosperity, and their years in pleasures*

SCRIPTURAL GUARANTEES FOR YOUR FINANCIAL ABUNDANCE

1. Financial abundance is God's agenda for the end-time church. *Joel 2:21-28.* No one in Zion is permitted to live in financial shame or misfortune. The end-time church is meant to be a reigning church and not a defeated church. One of the boosters of the end-time church reign is financial dominion. God will be unleashing financial fortune upon the end-time church. It is written in *Haggai 2:8-9. The silver is mine, and the gold is mine, saith the LORD of hosts. The glory of this latter house (end-time church) shall be greater than of the former, saith the LORD of hosts.*
2. Financial abundance is our heritage in Abrahamic covenant. *Genesis 22:17-18. Galatians 3:29.* That every child of God is a seed of Abraham is the proper description of dominion. *Genesis 12:1-3. Now the Lord had said unto Abram, Get thee out of thy country, and from thy kindred, and from thy father's house, unto a land that I will shew thee: And I will make of thee a great nation, and I will bless thee, and make thy name great; and thou shalt be a blessing: And I will bless them that bless thee, and curse him that curseth thee: and in thee shall all families of the earth be blessed.*

We have access to the DNA of financial dominion and prosperity. You possess the same DNA as Abraham. So in the DNA of Abraham is the DNA of greatness and of blessings that are not just financial. *Galatians 3:26-29.* There is no limitation to your greatness (v28). Vs. 29 speaks of seed, offspring, and descendants. And so, flowing in my veins is the capacity to be a blessing. Hence, *Genesis 12* belongs to you and me.

3. The first thing God did when he created man was to bless him. He did not create man and curse him, but rather, he blessed man with the empowerment to be fruitful. *Genesis 1:28.*

WHAT IS FINANCIAL ABUNDANCE?

1. The ability to totally conquer lack, poverty, financial hardship and the effects they create.
2. Financial dominion is having mastery over money and wealth.
3. It is to be abundantly supplied, free from debt, and becoming a blessing to others.
4. It is living the blessed and the abundant life where your financial needs are met through covenant provisions, and you are able to meet the needs of others. *Genesis 12:2.*

PRAYERS THAT CHANGE FINANCIAL PROBLEMS PERPETUALLY

2 Corinthians 9:6. Father make me a carrier of these graces. Father, I ask that you enlarge my capacity for financial faith today.

1. **Financial anointing:** Having money begins not with cash, but with having financial anointing. Money responds to the anointing; and just as there is an anointing for healing,

there is also anointing for finances and wealth creation. *Jesus and Peter. Matthew 17:27*. Once it rests on you, your destiny changes for good. Financial anointing is the opposite of a curse/jinx; the latter being the enablement that people carry that ruins everything for them. Although it is also an anointing, it is a negative one. When a curse is placed on a person, it places a force on a person that does not allow anything to work out. Instead, the financial anointing is called "the blessing"(not blessings). It is the seed, and blessings are the fruits. That is what Abraham had. Wherever you go, money flows. It is called the anointing for blessings. That is what is on this commission. It is a non-negotiable resource.

2. The faith for finances (**Financial faith**). Ask for enlargement of faith for finance. God has dealt for everyone a measure of faith. *Romans 12:3*. Ask for increasing measure of faith. There is faith in the realm of 100s, in the realm of 1000s, and in the realm of millions. Even when you carry the anointing, you need financial faith. Even if you have been functioning in it, ask for your faith to be renewed. Nothing refreshes faith like hearing freshly from God. Fellowship with God. You do not pray for faith, but rather, a greater capacity to believe.

3. **Financial wisdom.** There is wisdom for wealth creation. When you lack it, you will always be broke. Even when your faith attracts it. what faith and anointing attract, it is wisdom that preserves it. Solomon prayed for it. That's why you need messages on financial wisdom. Jesus Christ is the power of God and the wisdom of God. *Proverbs 8:15, 18-19. By me kings reign, and princes decree justice. Riches and honor are with me; yea, durable riches and righteousness. My fruit is better than gold, yea, than fine gold; and my revenue than choice silver. Ecclesiastes 7:12. Wisdom is a shelter as money is a shelter, but the advantage of knowledge is this: Wisdom preserves those who have it*

4. **Financial favor.** Favor will give you far more than your labor can give you. Favor causes men to get involved in your life with their resources. *Exodus 12:36 [ESV]. And the Lord had given the people favor in the sight of the Egyptians, so that they let them have what they asked. Thus they plundered the Egyptians.* It is seed that unlocks favor. 1 Corinthians 9:6.
5. **Financial channels.** Human beings - not angels - are channels of money. They are the channels to bring things to your life. Jesus said, men shall give to your bosom. You need pillars. You need men. You have to pray for men and women to get involved in your life and in your ventures, and for the presence of wealth-carrying laborers in your vineyard. There are certain seasons in your life when God opens channels and places people in your life to take care of you. *Luke 8:1-2.*

Day 13. *Victorious thought for the day.* Salvation does not only guarantee the forgiveness of your sins; it also provides for your financial prosperity.

PRAYERS

Father, I receive the wisdom for wealth creation and financial abundance

By the authority in the name of Jesus, whatever I lay my hands upon shall prosper and flourish.

By the power of God's word, I will not labor in vain. The yoke of toiling and laboring without result is broken from my life.

My father, I pray that you will make me financially blessed to become a blessing to my family, to your church and to my generation.

My father, I pray for financial favor upon my life that the fruit of my life will not be by labor only but by your favor.

Day 14

I AM RESTORED BY COVENANT

DAY 14
I AM RESTORED BY COVENANT

This is your day of total restoration of destiny. There shall be restoration of health, finance, relationships and opportunities. *Exodus 2:23-25*

John 10:10. While the devil is in the ministry of taking, killing and destroying, God in his infinite grace is in the ministry of saving, giving, and restoring. *1 John 3:8*.

THINGS TO KNOW AND CONSIDER

1. First thing you must know is that God is a God of restoration. God is a God of restoration. There is nothing stolen that redemption has not restored. *Joel 2:25-26. And I will restore to you the years that the locust hath eaten, the cankerworm, and the caterpillar, and the palmerworm, my great army which I sent among you. ²⁶ And ye shall eat in plenty, and be satisfied, and praise the name of the Lord your God, that hath dealt wondrously with you: and my people shall never be ashamed.*
2. Secondly, when God speaks of recovery, it usually involves two major things. It means the "taking back of what the enemy stole from you," and the "taking back of what the enemy held back from you." There are things that belong to you, that Satan is preventing you from obtaining.

For example, the land belonged to the Israelites, but their fear of the giants prevented them from entering the land.

3. Thirdly, whenever God restores, the recovery does not take place at the level of the lost. God restores better and in greater capacity than whatever you lost. David and his men did not just get what the enemy took from them. The thief already took from Judah, the philistines and other cities of Caleb. So when David recovered all, it was more than what he lost. God restores in plenty. You will eat in plenty and be satisfied and magnify the name of the Lord who has dealt wondrously with you.

Job 42:10. And the Lord turned the captivity of Job, when he prayed for his friends: also the Lord gave Job twice as much as he had before. Then came there unto him all his brethren, and all his sisters, and all they that had been of his acquaintance before, and did eat bread with him in his house: and they bemoaned him, and comforted him over all the evil that the Lord had brought upon him: every man also gave him a piece of money, and everyone an earring of gold. So the Lord blessed the latter end of Job more than his beginning: for he had fourteen thousand sheep, and six thousand camels, and a thousand yoke of oxen, and a thousand she asses. He also had seven sons and three daughters. And in all the land were no women found so fair as the daughters of Job: and their father gave them inheritance among their brethren.

I recover in ten-folds all my wasted years in Jesus name.

4. Fourth, one of the platforms for destiny restoration is the covenant. After over 400 years in captivity and slavery, God remembered his covenant with Abraham, Isaac and with Jacob, and rescued the destinies of the Israelites. *2 Samuel 9:1. And David said, Is there yet any that is left of the house of Saul, that I may shew him kindness for Jonathan's sake?*

WHEN COVENANT IS AT WORK

Whenever covenant is at work, three things usually happen.

1. **Covenant will remember you.** Generationally, Mephibosheth was a forgotten man left in Lodebar to suffer the consequences of his grandfather's action. People had forgotten him. Society left him as an outcast, but covenant cried on his behalf. Whenever a new king takes over from one king, he usually kills everyone left in the house of his predecessor. Therefore, Mephibosheth had a death sentence hanging over his head. God is a covenant-keeping God. *Psalms 89:34 My covenant will I not break, nor alter the thing that has gone out of my lips.* Mephibosheth was lifted beyond generational limitations. God had also rejected him and his seed from having access to a life of honor; but covenant remembered him. *Psalms 105:42. For he remembers his holy promise and Abraham his servant. He brought out his people with joy, His chosen ones with gladness. He gave them the lands of the Gentiles and they inherited the labor of the nations.* In *Esther 6:1*, the destiny of Mordecai was delivered and restored on the platform of covenant. He was remembered and the gallows experience was averted. In *Genesis 8:1, God remembered Noah, and every living thing, and all the cattle that was with him in the ark: and God made a wind to pass over the earth, and the waters assuaged.* Galatians 3:13, 14, 29. What are your sacrifices yet to be rewarded? What are your prayers that are yet to be answered? Where you have no voice, he raises people to speak for you. *1 Samuel 16:18. Then answered one of the servants, and said, Behold, I have seen a son of Jesse the Bethlehemite, that is cunning in playing, and a mighty valiant man, and a man of war, and prudent in matters, and a comely person, and the Lord is with him.*

2. **Covenant will relocate you.** Covenant does not leave you where it meets you. It changes your status. Mephibosheth's shame of living in Lodebar, hanging out with the nobodies, ended on that day. Mordecai moved from being a gate man to riding on a royal horse. No matter the limitation holding people back, covenant will relocate you and lift you and me above any earthly limitations. There are all kinds of limitations: geographical, governmental, territorial, people, etc. Covenant is never between people with similar strengths or similar weaknesses. God instituted a parallel for mankind in the marriage covenant - Jesus Christ married a church that was weak and imperfect with the aim of making her reach perfection, power and influence.

3. **Covenant reimburses you.** When covenant is at work for your restoration, it causes you to be reimbursed. All your accrued blessings and benefits will be released. There will be a total recovery of lost dignity, glory and properties. *2 Samuel 9:7 And David said unto him, Fear not: for I will surely shew thee kindness for Jonathan thy father's sake, and will restore thee all the land of Saul thy father; and thou shalt eat bread at my table continually. Esther 6:3. And the king said, what honor and dignity hath been done to Mordecai for this? Then said the king's servants that ministered unto him, there is nothing done for him.* Covenant also benefits your children's children. Covenant gives you an edge. *2 Samuel 9:13. So Mephibosheth dwelt in Jerusalem: for he did eat continually at the king's table; and was lame on both his feet.*

WHAT DO YOU HAVE TO DO?

Believe, obey, and plead the covenant. When Judah pleaded the covenant, God gave him rest all around. *2 Chronicles 25:12, 15. And they entered into a covenant to seek the LORD God of their fathers with all their heart and with all their soul; ...And all Judah rejoiced at* *the oath: for they had sworn with all their heart, and sought him with their whole desire; and he was found of them: and the LORD gave them rest round about.* Keeping the conditions of the covenant will commit God to perform on our behalf.

You need to develop a covenant exception mentality. *Ezekiel 9:6. Slay utterly old and young, both maids, and little children, and women: but come not near any man upon whom is the mark; and begin at my sanctuary. Then they began at the ancient men which were before the house.*

Day 14: *Victorious thought for the day.* Covenant does not leave you where it meets you. Covenant will always remember, relocate and reimburse you.

PRAYERS.

My father, my father, the God that remembered Rachael and Noah, remember me in this season to open doors for my destiny restoration and elevation.

Wherever I am located that is contrary to divine destiny, I pray that the mighty hand of God will relocate me by the covenant in the blood of Jesus.

The God who forcefully delivered the Israelites from the grip of Pharaoh in Egypt, arise and deliver my destiny from the grip of any stubborn oppressor in Jesus name.

By the power in the blood of Jesus, I decree that mind is restored, my finance is restored, and my health is restored.

Day 15

I SHALL EAT THE GOOD OF THE LAND

DAY 15
I SHALL EAT THE GOOD OF THE LAND

Isaiah 1:19. If ye be willing and obedient, ye shall eat the good of the land.

One of the marks of manifestations is access to the good of the land. God has reserved the good of the land for his children including you and I and this is our season to embrace them. We are going to exercise our faith prayerfully to enjoy the good of the land. Your heavenly father has by redemption, laid up an inheritance for you, and this is your season to embrace the good of the land.

Joshua 1:1-8. Psalms 24:1. By these scriptures, God is the authentic owner of the earth and its fullness. And one of the rights of ownership is the power of delegation or the ability to transfer ownership. Since God is the owner and the landlord of everything, you only need his permission for possession. Therefore, that you are approved to possess and enjoy the good of the land, is in line with divine mandate. *Joshua 1:1-8.* This is your season to take territories, inherit your inheritance, and possess your possessions. *1 Corinthians 10:6* From the testimonies of the scripture, Israel is the type of the church. Israel was delivered from Egypt in order to inherit Canaan, the land of promise. Egypt is the type of the world, our old lives before Christ, which we have been delivered from in order for us to embrace the Canaan-like experience.

SIGNIFICANCE OF CANAAN/THE TERRITORIES TO THE BELIEVER

For the Israelites, it actually meant physical land; but for us Christians, it includes – but is much more than - physical land. Our territories or the lands that we are to possess are "all the blessings and privileges that belong to us in Christ Jesus."

Redemption is an all-rounded supernatural experience, which is not limited to salvation from sin alone. Although, receiving forgiveness for our sins should not be taken lightly because it is the fundamental requirement into the new life. Establishing the proper relationship with God through the finished work of Christ is the foundation for possessing our possessions. However, as believers in Christ, there are other benefits that we need to know and pursue. Inheritance of spiritual redemption, economic redemption, godly family heritage, good health, divine protection, longevity, possessing physical territories, etc. *1 Peter 1:3, 4 KJV. Psalms 2:8. Deuteronomy 28:1-13.*

Prayerfully embrace the seven-fold covenant blessing in *Deuteronomy 28:1-13.*

1. GEOGRAPHICAL HERITAGE BLESSING. *Vs. 3 & 6. Isaiah 54:2*
2. OCCUPATIONAL HERITAGE BLESSING. *Deuteronomy 28:4, 5 & 11, Zechariah 8:13 [NLT].*
3. INHERITANCE OF SUPERNATURAL VICTORY *Vs. 7. Isaiah 54:17*
4. INHERITANCE OF SUPERNATURAL ELEVATION. *Vs. 13.*
5. INHERITANCE OF FINANCIAL PROSPERITY. *Vs. 4 & 12.*
6. INHERITANCE OF FAMILY HERITAGE AND GOOD HEALTH. *Vs. 9 & 10.*
7. INHERITANCE OF SUPERNATURAL FAVOR. *Vs. 12.*

WHAT DO YOU DO TO EAT THE GOOD OF THE LAND?

1. **You must be willing.** God does not force anything on people. Willingness means carefully consenting, with readiness, hunger, passion. Having a desire that is stronger than the opposition. Do not allow past or present disappointments to discourage or sabotage your faith. Seek God passionately in the word, in prayer, and fellowship. Your willingness should compel you to have a workable plan. Plan like never before, to accomplish big things in this season and beyond. Go as far as the favor of God will take you.

2. **Step in by faith.** *Numbers 13:30. And Caleb stilled the people before Moses, and said, Let us go up at once, and possess it; for we are well able to overcome it.* Caleb agreed with God in faith. Usually there can be two responses. One of faith and the other of fear. There is the response of "we are well more than able" and that of "we are unable." All of our inheritances in God are received by faith. Therefore by faith, press for your healing, your deliverance, your marital breakthrough and your financial abundance. The ones you will possess are the ones you go after. In the same manner that the Israelites encountered obstacles such as the Red Sea, the armies of Pharaoh, the wilderness, River Jordan, the wall of Jericho and the giants, you will also be confronted with obstacles. However, with the force of faith, every challenge can be a springboard to usher you into your next dimension. Those who procrastinate and never decide and plan for conquest will never obtain their inheritance.

3. **You have to have the** type of spirit in Caleb. It is called the possibility mentality. It is the **spirit of faith**. It is the spirit that believes in God to a point where you step out on the strength of His instructions. *Numbers 14:24. But my servant Caleb, because he had another spirit with him, and hath followed*

me fully, him will I bring into the land where into he went; and his seed shall possess it. As a result of this spirit, the entire generation that doubted God for their inheritance died in the wilderness with the exception of Caleb and Joshua.

4. **Obedience**. Progress in the kingdom requires receiving and obeying instructions. *Deuteronomy 28:1*. Operating as per divine instructions and directions. Obedience in seed faith-giving. Do not let the devil intimidate you to back down from seed faith-giving at such a critical time in your life, so that favor can be at work for you. Know that there are supernatural interventions, which only your sacrificial obedience will bring.

5. **Place value on instruction and directions.** Job 36:11. Whatsoever he asked you to do, do it.

6. **Make room for the Holy Spirit in your life.** The supernatural is necessary for your success. Jesus' success in life was tied to the person and the power of the Holy Spirit. Until the Holy Spirit came upon Jesus at the Jordan River after baptism, he never preached or performed a miracle. *Acts 10:38, Acts 1:1-2.* Praying in the spirit. There are dimensions of wisdom and operational strategies required to set you above others which is only possible through the Holy Spirit.

7. **Put the past behind you**. *Isaiah 43:18-19*. In life, we are bound to miss our targets at one time or the other. Failures we do not envisage do happen, sometimes; so do disappointments, unfulfilled dreams, etc. These are some of the things you might have encountered in your recent past. Were there mistakes you have made recently? Are there goals you have been unable to accomplish? Were there missed targets and disappointments? Life is such that after every mistake, failure, or even success, there must be a re-

focusing. You must constantly focus and refocus. Whoever wants to do better refocusing, must put the past behind. No one looks back and forward at the same time.

Day 15: *Victorious thought for the day.* Always remember that redemption has reserved the good of the land for you.

PRAYERS

My heavenly father, I pray that you will open my eyes of understanding to discover my inheritance in Christ. That my eyes will be open to the wonderful things God has prepared for me in the land.

My father, my father, guide me today and always, into the prepared blessings you have reserved for me. *Psalms 23.*

In the name of Jesus, I decree that every force coming against my inheritance is shattered

I decree that I overcome every opposing force, opposing power resisting my flourishing in the land by the blood of Jesus. *Revelation 12:11.*

Day 16

RISING ABOVE THE LIMITATIONS OF LIFE FOR A NEW LEVEL OF RESULTS

DAY 16
RISING ABOVE THE LIMITATIONS OF LIFE FOR A NEW LEVEL OF RESULTS

I am convinced in my spirit that from today, helpers will show up for you. Every helper that you need to succeed in life, shall begin to show up for you. Prayerfully say, "Father, let helpers from expected and unexpected quarters locate me daily in this season. Whatever human helper that I need in order to go forward, let them locate me. Whatever human helper that I need for my promotion and elevation, let them locate me. Command them to locate me. Every helper needed by my children, let them locate me. My father, my father, all those who are waiting to see me fail; waiting to mock my failing, they will wait in vain. Peninah waited continuously to mock Hannah but the lifter showed up and lifted Hannah. All those who are waiting to mock you in the valley of failure, shall wait in vain. The power that lifted Jesus from the grave will lift you out of stagnancy in this season, in Jesus name.

Luke 19:1-9. Then Jesus entered and passed through Jericho. Now behold, there was a man named Zacchaeus who was a chief tax collector, and he was rich. And he sought to see who Jesus was, but could not because of the crowd, for he was of short stature. So he ran ahead and climbed up into a sycamore tree to see Him, for He was going to pass that way. And when Jesus came to the place, He looked up and saw him, and said to him, "Zacchaeus, make haste and come down, for today I must stay at your house." So he made haste and came down, and received Him joyfully. But when they saw it, they all complained, saying, "He has gone to be a guest with a man who is a sinner."

Then Zacchaeus stood and said to the Lord, "Look, Lord, I give half of my goods to the poor; and if I have taken anything from anyone by false accusation, I restore four-fold. And Jesus said to him, "Today salvation has come to this house, because he is also a son of Abraham; for the Son of Man has come to seek and to save that which was lost.

Zacchaeus wanted to experience a new level of result that he never experienced before. Even though, he was a rich man, yet he was poor. He wanted to experience true riches. There is a difference between being rich and flourishing. *Mark 8:36*. All his life he had been accumulating worldly riches, running after the mundane things of life.

We have established that a life of impact is more than having things even though it includes having things. The success of any child of God should not be measured by material possessions, but by societal impact. Just like everyone of us, Zacchaeus wanted a redirection, but he had limitations. He desired to secure the attention of Jesus Christ but had some constraints. He wanted to see glory, but had obstacles. He wanted to encounter the supernatural, but there were forces limiting him. Whatever is hindering you from experiencing glory shall be paralyzed today, in Jesus name.

The three major limitations in the life of Zacchaeus that constituted barriers to a flourishing life of impact and evidence were his small stature; the great crowd; and his profession as a tax collector which was regarded as sinful. A tax collector at that time was regarded as the one who became rich through corrupt practices. So, society placed a tag on his life, that he did not qualify to be a friend of God. What are the limiting factors or barriers in your life today? How did Zacchaeus overcome the barriers confronting him?

First thing he did was to run and climb atop the sycamore tree. There were other trees in that place, so why the sycamore tree? It was the tallest of the trees. That is, he took a path that would make him stand out in life.

What was the sycamore tree and what is your sycamore tree today? A barrier breaker.

A limitation quencher. A ladder of lifting. The push needed to escape from undesirable situations and circumstances. A destiny enhancer. When he climbed the sycamore tree, he put the crowd under him. The crowd would have stopped him and even stepped on him. May God show you your sycamore tree and give you the power to climb it, in Jesus name.

Your prayer today is that God should show you your own limitation quencher, the ladder you need to climb, and connect you with your destiny enhancers so you can move to your next level.

FOUR THINGS HAPPENED TO HIM

1. He was properly located, which made him stand out and become prominent.
2. He rose above the crowd and put the crowd (his obstacles) underneath him.
3. He secured the attention of Jesus.
4. Jesus, the carrier of grace visited him. David said, "goodness and mercy shall follow me." I see angel goodness and mercy following you home. *Psalms 23.*

HOW DO I RISE ABOVE LIMITATIONS?

1. **Know your limitations.** Zacchaeus knew who he was. Know your strength. He knew he was short. There was a

crowd and he was a sinner. Know your own problem. What is your weakness? Do you sleep too much? Are you prayerless? Ask God to open your eyes to see your strengths and weaknesses.

2. **Decide to change.** It is difficult, but that is the only way to move on. If there is something you are doing and you know it is not allowing you to go forward, stop it. Let those who steal, steal no more. *Ephesians 4:28. Anyone who has been stealing must steal no longer, but must work, doing something useful with their own hands, that they may have something to share with those in need.* Let those who are angry, be angry no more. Let those who are prayerless, become prayerful.

3. **You must press harder in life.** Zacchaeus ran to climb the sycamore tree. It was hard work to look for the tallest tree and climb it. Stop doing small things; look for audacious goals to achieve. Set huge goals for yourself. If at the end you didn't achieve it, you will know that you have tried. Whatever level, you are now, you must aspire to go higher. Those who do not aspire, will soon expire. The four lepers *in 2 Kings 7:3-10 said, if we sit down here, we will die here.* It is better to rise up, find a sycamore tree to climb than to remain lost in the crowd.

4. **By all means keep moving**. Someone said, if you cannot fly, run. If you cannot run, walk. If you cannot walk, crawl, but by all means, keep moving. Whatever your limitation may be, there is a strength in you for your lifting. *Ephesians 3:10.* Power of potential. Power of your dream. There is an inner potential in you. Yes, Zacchaeus was short, but he pulled his inner potential to see his tree and to climb it. If you are already born again, you must ask, have I been water baptized. If you are water baptized, you must aspire to be baptized in the Holy Spirit. If you are reading one Christian book in a month, you must ask yourself, when

will I begin to read two Christian books in a month? If you are winning one soul, you need to ask yourself, why not two?. Life must be progressively progressive, otherwise death is inevitable. You must not remain at the same level of life. If you have been praying for 20 minutes, you need to ask yourself, why not 40 minutes? You must make up your mind that you must not remain the same.

5. **Dare to be different.** You need to take some steps that look so crazy and mad, if you must experience glory. It must have looked crazy for a rich man to climb a sycamore tree. His colleagues going to the same club house must have been mocking him that day, wondering if Zacchaeus lost his mind. Is Zacchaeus mad? Why is he climbing the sycamore tree? Beloved, you need to make up your mind to be different, to dare to be different in this end-time. You need to do some things out of status quo if you want to flourish in these last days. In the realm of the spirit, the ridiculous sometimes produces the miracle.

6. **Make progressive relationships.** *Luke 8:1-2.* Are your friends pillars or caterpillars? Pillars will raise you and caterpillars will break you down. Jesus had friends that were pillars to his destiny. Father, in this season, I connect with and embrace relationships that will be pillars to my destiny, in Jesus name.

Failures of my father's house and failures of my mother's house, I disconnect from you now, in the name of Jesus.

Day 16: *Victorious thought for the day.* The limitation you permit is the limitation that will be. Redemption has lifted you above all the limits of life.

PRAYERS

By the supernatural power that lifted Jesus from the grave, my destiny is lifted above any barrier standing against my destiny in Jesus name.

I invoke the power of the blood of Jesus that my destiny cannot be limited, will not be limited, and shall never be limited.

I decree by the power in the name of Jesus that every force operating to suppress my destiny, oppress my destiny, and limit my progress, is shattered forever.

As the grave could not hold Jesus back, nothing shall forever be able from holding me back from fulfilling destiny in Jesus name.

Day 17

I EMBRACE DIRECTION FOR MY MANIFESTATIONS

DAY 17
I EMBRACE DIRECTION FOR MY MANIFESTATIONS

Deuteronomy 32:9-13. For the Lord's portion is his people; Jacob is the lot of his inheritance. He found him in a desert land, and in the waste howling wilderness; he led him about, he instructed him, he kept him as the apple of his eye. As an eagle stirreth up her nest, fluttereth over her young, spreadeth abroad her wings, taketh them, beareth them on her wings: So the Lord alone did lead him, and there was no strange god with him. He made him ride on the high places of the earth, that he might eat the increase of the fields; and he made him to suck honey out of the rock, and oil out of the flinty rock... It is our destiny to be in high places. Not by human arrangements, but by divine arrangement. To every place there is a path. It is the path you follow that determines the way you will end.

One of the benefits of an encounter is access to divine direction. Also, one of the benefits of fasting and prayer is access to divine direction. *Isaiah 8:11. And the Lord shall guide thee continually, and satisfy thy soul in drought, and make fat thy bones: and thou shalt be like a watered garden, and like a spring of water, whose waters fail not.*

Direction is key to acceleration. The worst thing that can happen to anybody is to travel fast in the wrong direction. Speed is a waste when the direction is wrong. The greatest problem of man is direction. Life becomes a burdensome task in the absence of proper direction. It will be a life where everybody is trying to do what everybody is doing, with continued frustration. Lack of direction is thus the gateway to affliction.

Only the led will ever take the lead. Jesus met Peter as ordinary fisherman in *Matthew 4:19*, but by following divine direction, he became a foremost Apostle. With divine direction from God telling you to go ahead, you will become the head. The end is secured for the led. When you are led, your journey cannot be terminated. You cannot be afraid of tomorrow, when you follow his leading for your life. When he leads you, he will work for you. *1 Thessalonians 5:24*. When he leads you he will keep you. So, if you want God to be committed in keeping you, be committed in following him.

In this life, opportunity appeals to us whether good or bad. There are things that look like gold but in reality are garbage. Dangerous smooth talkers abound. Some speak to you about marriage, but they are demonic, dangerous women who want to ensnare you, and your brain is inadequate to sort out the deception of this life.

Laban cheated Jacob for 20 years until one day God showed Jacob the way out. *Genesis 31*. Some jobs can look very attractive, but they are not from God. May your eyes and ears reject anything not from God that Satan is deceptively showing to you.

There are 4 dimensions through which God can give you direction for promotion.

1. **He gives you vision for the future.** Habakkuk 2:1-2. I will stand upon my watch and set me upon the tower, and will watch to see what he will say unto me, and what I shall answer when I am reproved. This refers to God's plan and

purpose for your life. His plan for you today, tomorrow, and in the future.
2. **He gives you direction for daily living.** This covers practically everything regarding guidance for your daily living. Where to live? Who to marry and who not to marry? Should you travel or not? Directions to avoid danger, and to embrace daily provisions. Do not assume anything; inquire about everything.
3. Proverbs 3:5-7. Trust in the Lord with all thine heart; and lean not unto thine own understanding. In all thy ways acknowledge him, and he shall direct thy paths. Be not wise in thine own eyes: fear the Lord, and depart from evil. Jeremiah 6:16. Thus saith the Lord, Stand ye in the ways, and see, and ask for the old paths, where is the good way, and walk therein, and ye shall find rest for your souls. But they said, We will not walk therein.
4. **Revelation and wisdom for profitable living.** How to live a life that is profitable and fruitful. In your career, your business, your ministry or in whatever you do. What are the steps to take in order to be profitable? 1 Kings 3:5-9. Prayer for guidance, centers around inquiry. Father should I go? Should I invest? David was a mighty warrior, but he understood that the mighty could fall. He would always make inquiries of the Lord. Do not assume anything; inquire about everything.
5. **Revelations of mysteries.** Hidden secrets. There are things related to your destiny that you do not know that you must know. Jeremiah 33:3. Call unto me, and I will answer thee, and show thee great and mighty things, which thou knows not [NLT]. Ask me and I will tell you some remarkable secrets about what is going to happen here.

How to connect to divine guidance.

1. You must desire to be divinely guided. What you do not desire, you do not deserve. There are dangers on your journey of life, but when guided, it takes away your fear. *Psalms 23:5.*
2. You must recognize that God is committed to guide you. *Psalms 32:8. John 10:4-5.*
3. You must engage the channels of prayer and fasting in facilitating your following. *Jeremiah 33:3.* Moses prayed 3 major prayers. *Exodus 33:3.* Lord show me the way. Follow me with your presence. Show me your glory.

This season, God will show you a vision, a revelation, a voice that will grant you breakthrough. Say boldly; "I REFUSE TO BE CONFUSED. My father, my father, position my destiny by divine direction for supernatural supplies. I WILL ALWAYS BE DIVINELY LOCATED FOR PRESERVATION AND PROVISION."

Day 17: *Victorious thought for the day.* Whenever God leads you, no man can mislead you.

PRAYERS

Father, I will walk in agreement with your plans and purpose for me throughout the rest of my life. I will be on course for the rest of my life.

Father, I ask that you unveil your plans and purpose for me, and I will never miss your plans for my life.

Father, help me to experience step by step directions for daily living. I will not be in the wrong places with the wrong people. But will be at the right place, at the right time, with the right people, doing the right things and obtaining the right outcomes.

Father, I connect with wisdom for profitable living.

I connect with revelations for mysteries to be made known to me. Open my eyes to know whatever is a hidden mystery around my life.

Father make known to me why things may not be working in my life now.

Father, open my eyes to see and know whatever is causing me to experience delay and dryness in any area of my life.

Father; thank you that nothing is hidden anymore to me about my life.

Day 18

THIS IS MY NEW DAY: MY SEASON OF NEWNESS

DAY 18
THIS IS MY NEW DAY: MY SEASON OF NEWNESS

Revelations 21:5. And he that sat upon the throne said, Behold, I make all things new. And he said unto me, Write: for these words are true and faithful.

Isaiah 43:18-19. Remember ye not the former things, neither consider the things of old. Behold, I will do a new thing; now it shall spring forth; shall ye not know it? I will even make a way in the wilderness, and rivers in the desert.

Welcome to your day of newness and new beginnings. It is the dawn of a new era in your life. A time of spiritual vitality, and refreshing from the presence of God. *Acts 3:19.* A time that you and I will experience new levels of joy, unusual promotions, testimonies, miracles and newer dimensions of breakthroughs.

Our God is a God of new beginnings. In *Genesis 1*, He started the earth all over again. In Genesis chapters 3,6 and 9, he gave man the chance for a new beginning. In Lamentations 3:22-23, he promises to give new mercies every day. In *Micah.7:8*, he promises you and I a new hope of rising up whenever we fall or fail. For those who are lost and confused, God promises them the opportunity of a new life in *John 3:3-4*.

In the dictionary, renewal means to replace or repair something that is worn out, run-down, or broken. However, God defines renewal and newness in two different dimensions:

1. God makes anew what is old and worn out. Isaiah 43:18-19. Remember ye not the former things, neither consider the things of old. Behold, I will do a new thing; now it shall spring forth; shall ye not know it? I will even make a way in the wilderness, and rivers in the desert.

What is humanly considered worthless, old and worn out can be re-energized and empowered with the breath of God to become anew. God provides meaning to a meaningless life. Instead of a worn-out body, he renews your youth like the eagle's. By his divine renewal, a dirt-poor man can become a financial champion. He breathes into a relationship that is hopeless and meaningless and bring joy out of it. With his act of newness, God changed the destiny of Naomi and brought joy out of her bitter experience. By an encounter with the living God, we have seen a total transformation in the lives of those that society had given up on. Hardened criminals that the correctional system failed to rehabilitate have been changed drastically to become great citizens of their nations. Diseased organs have been - revitalized and healed by the power of God despite the negative prediction of medical science. A woman with multiple sclerosis walked into one of our services mid-last year with a walking cane. After being ministered to and upon the next visit to her physician, she was totally declared healed. She has since been walking and doing what she could not do before. Child of God, this is your hour to experience divine renewal in Jesus name.

2. Secondly, God also brings renewal and newness by creating what has never been created before. The fact that something has never been done before does not mean that it cannot be achieved. God specializes in bringing to existence for the first time what is yet to exist. That something

is not in existence or has never been completed before, does not intimidate God. *"Since the world began was it not heard that any man opened the eyes of one that was born blind"* John 9:32. When God opened the eyes of this young man who was born blind, he became the first one in his community to experience such manifestation. This month, I see you experiencing such order of miracles that have never been seen before in Jesus name.

HOW DO YOU EMBRACE THE NEWNESS OF GOD FOR YOUR LIFE?

1. **Consider a new way of thinking.**

   Until the pattern of the old is broken, it is impossible to embrace the new. Matthew 9:17. New wine must be place in a new wine skin. Embracing the possibility and the ability of God anew, requires that you and I must think correctly. No one rises beyond his or her level of thinking, because your thinking creates your reality. *Proverbs 23:7*. You cannot think defeat and expect victory. You cannot think sick and expect to be in good health and wellness. You cannot think poor and expect to enjoy abundance. No matter what confronts you, let your thinking be rooted in God's word for your life. Romans 12:1-2.

2. **Consider a new way of doing things.**

   It is not enough to align your thinking with God's plan for your life; you must also align your actions. *John 2:5. Whatever he tells you to do, do it.* Throughout this month, prayerfully take steps and embark on actions that will be congruent with God's plan and congruent with your expectations. Your prayer life must be at the level of your expectations. Your giving life must be different and must align with the level of your expectations. Obedience in tithing, seed sowing, and generous giving is a must in order to see the manifestations of His newness in your finances.

3. **Be prepared to encounter God daily.**

   In *Genesis 32:22-30*, Jacob encountered God at Peniel and experienced total renewal in the presence of God. He experienced a change of name, a change of character and a change of destiny. God changed his destiny from just a person to a nation. *Genesis 32:28. And he said, Thy name shall be called no more Jacob, but Israel: for as a prince hast thou power with God and with men, and hast prevailed.* No one encounters God and remains unchanged. Whenever you encounter God, He deals with your foundations and uproots whatever is hindering the manifestations of your success. **Until we are broken, we cannot be truly blessed.**

   Peniel represents the place of purging. It is the place where we give up in order to go up. It is a place where you surrender to the Lord all your plans and schemes so He can lead and lift you. It is the place where you finally see God and recognize your utter dependence on him. All his life, Jacob had been a trickster or deceiver, totally living up to the meaning of his name. He constantly manipulated and schemed to try to make the circumstances of life go his way. But at Peniel, he came face-to-face with God and had a radical change of heart. Like Jacob, we must bring ourselves to God to break us daily, on the altar of repentance, prayer, and the word of God.

4. **Renewal is on the platform of repentance.**

   Spiritual renewal and vitality occurs in our lives when we are quick to repent of our sins. Sin is a blocker of the move of God in any life. Repent of your sins so you can enjoy spiritual vitality and refreshing. *Acts 3:19 [NKJV]. Repent therefore and be converted, that your sins may be blotted out, so that times of refreshing may come from the presence of the Lord...*

5. Revitalize your prayer life.

Bring the fire back on your prayer altar. With a fervent altar of prayer, you can turn every trial to testimony. You can turn every mockery into miracles. It was the altar of fervent prayer that broke the yoke of years of barrenness in the life of Hannah. 1 Samuel 1:13. Hannah was praying in her heart, and her lips were moving but her voice was not heard. Eli thought she was drunk. Be watchful, alert and spiritually sensitive this month and beyond.

Mathew 13:24-25. Another parable He put forth to them, saying: "The kingdom of heaven is like a man who sowed good seed in his field; but while men slept, his enemy came and sowed tares among the wheat and went his way.

Spiritual slothfulness and prayerlessness are gateways for satanic havoc in any life. Make up your mind this month to increase your prayer life. Choose to talk more to God about your life, than to man. Pray for the full manifestation of God's plan for your life, your family, your church, your pastors, and your nation.

6. Embrace your newness by beholding God's word

2 Corinthians 3:18. You become what you behold. As you behold God's word daily, the Holy Spirit changes you are into God's image. You become strengthened, empowered and fortified for total victory. You are transformed from fear to faith. Transformed from cowardice to courage. Rest assured this month, that it is not the devil or your circumstances that set the boundaries of what you can become. It is the word of God that sets the boundary of what you can become and experience. No situation can alter the validity of his words. No challenge can unsettle his word. *Romans 3;4. Let God be true and let all men be liars. Matthew 24:35, Luke 21:33. Heaven and earth shall pass away, but my words shall not pass away.*

Day 18: ***Victorious thought for the day.*** The God of newness is able to breath into your life for a new beginning.

PRAYERS

Isaiah 43:18-19. Remember ye not the former things, neither consider the things of old.[19] *Behold, I will do a new thing; now it shall spring forth; shall ye not know it? I will even make a way in the wilderness, and rivers in the desert.*

My father, my father, let the failures, the disappointments of the past months, and years, be rolled away in Jesus name.

In this new season, I pray that God will do something new in my life, in my family, in his church, and in this nation in Jesus name.

Father, let doors of opportunities, doors of progress, doors of good surprises open up for me this day and forever in Jesus name.

Day 19

I RECEIVE GRACE TO CONQUER WORRY AND ANXIETY

DAY 19
I RECEIVE GRACE TO CONQUER WORRY AND ANXIETY

HOW TO OVERCOME WORRY AND ANXIETY

Matthew 6:24-34. No man can serve two masters: for either he will hate the one, and love the other; or else he will hold to the one, and despise the other. Ye cannot serve God and mammon. Therefore I say unto you, Take no thought for your life, what ye shall eat, or what ye shall drink; nor yet for your body, what ye shall put on. Is not the life more than meat, and the body than raiment? Behold the fowls of the air: for they sow not, neither do they reap, nor gather into barns; yet your heavenly Father feedeth them. Are ye not much better than they? Which of you by taking thought can add one cubit unto his stature? And why take ye thought for raiment? Consider the lilies of the field, how they grow; they toil not, neither do they spin: And yet I say unto you, That even Solomon in all his glory was not arrayed like one of these. Wherefore, if God so clothe the grass of the field, which today is, and tomorrow is cast into the oven, shall he not much more clothe you, O ye of little faith? Therefore take no thought, saying, What shall we eat? or, What shall we drink? or, Wherewithal shall we be clothed? (For after all these things do the Gentiles seek:) for your heavenly Father knoweth that ye have need of all these things. But seek ye first the kingdom of God, and his righteousness; and all these things shall be added unto you. Take therefore no thought for the morrow: for the morrow shall take thought for the things of itself. Sufficient unto the day is the evil thereof.

We live in an age of anxiety. There are so many things happening in our world today, that can cause us to legitimately worry.

There are chronic diseases, threats from global issues such as terrorism, unfavorable governmental policies, personal problems, problems at your job, family matters, financial needs, health issues, problems with your family, the types of foods available in our time, etc. This is not how God wants us to live.

Worry is to mentally dwell on difficulty or trouble; it is a chronic concern and can turn into anxiety and fear. Anxiety is to be uneasy and nervous about an event, person or problem you cannot control, simply because it is out of your control.

There are also all kinds of worries. At the top of the list in a survey of middle-age Americans, is the worry about appearances, finances, and the fear of being audited by the Internal Revenue Service (IRS).

People worry about things that have already happened. This is very futile. Worrying about the past is like trying to put toothpaste back into the tube.

People worry over things that will inevitably happen. Some worry about growing old, but will grow old. Such are our attempts to change things we cannot control. *Matthew 16:27.* You cannot add any hour to your life, but you can cut it short.

Some people worry about things that will never happen. Surveys have shown that 80% of the things we worry about never happen. Dr. Walter Caver reported a survey on worry that indicated that only 8% of the things people worry about were legitimate matters of concern and the other 92% were imaginary and never happen.

Mark Twain once said, I have worried over a great many things in life, the most of which never happened. Worry is a type of fear; a fear of something imagined.

THE DANGERS OF WORRY

1. Worry and anxiety choke. The original English word for worry is "to choke." It paralyzes initiatives and kills the imagination.
2. Worry and anxiety create emotional distress, especially anxiety, which can create severe emotional distress. Anxiety can make us feel very restless, uncomfortable, and incapable of concentrating, so much so, that you might literally feel too distressed to work. Stress is the number one reason for sickness and disease. The number one reason for visiting the doctor's office is anxiety. Jesus told us not to worry and not to be anxious. 75 % to 95 % of all visits to primary care physicians are anxiety and stress-related disorders.
3. Worry does not empty tomorrow of its problems, it empties today of its strength. A theologian, Dr. Martyn Lloyd Jones said, "the result of worrying about the future is that you cripple yourself in the present." Worry and anxiety do not help your future but hurt your today, by denying you of the strength for the day. How many of you in worry add a cubit? *Matthew 6:27.*

The question is not whether you have a reason to be anxious, but rather, what you will do to manage it. How are you going to overcome it? Anxiety is a choice. How can you have a sense of peace when things are so difficult?

HOW TO OVERCOME WORRY & ANXIETY

1. **Believers should not worry.** Why? We are commanded in scripture not to worry, not to fear, and not to be anxious. God never created us to live in fear. God will never command us to do what we do not have the capacity to do. We have the ability to live without being anxious. As much as you know the presence of God by peace, you know the presence of the devil by fear. Not that you should not be concerned or think of the necessity of life. Not that you should not plan. However, do not be anxious about the issues of life.

   Worry can be a result of our failure to trust God to provide our needs. The root of all chronic fear, anxiety and worry is an orphan spirit. God is a faithful father who is trustworthy. Sometimes we simply do not understand the extent of God's love for us, and how good of a father, he is.

2. **Avoid living tomorrow, today.** While it is good to plan and have foresight be very mindful not to place upon yourself the burden of what will happen tomorrow. It is good to take ownership of your life, but you must always make allowance for the fact that you are not the sovereign God who is in control of yesterday, today and tomorrow. Jesus said in Matthew 6:34. *Therefore do not worry about tomorrow, for tomorrow will worry about itself. Each day has enough trouble of its own.* Plan, pray, and aggressively pursue your plans but leave the future outcome in the hands of the God who has the future in his hands. Plan for the future but maximize each day as a gift from God.

3. **Turn every anxious and worrisome thought into a prayer until victory.** Martin Luther said: pray and let God worry. You know God will not worry anyway, but the key there is, you have an assignment and God does. Yours is to never worry but to pray and trust. *Philippians 4:6-7. Do not*

be anxious about anything, but in every situation, by prayer and petition, with thanksgiving, present your requests to God. And the peace of God, which transcends all understanding, will guard your hearts and your minds in Christ Jesus. You either pray or worry. So when you are trying to pray religiously and worrisome thoughts keep coming, pray those thoughts. *1 Peter 5:7.*

4. With **thanksgiving** let your request mean that as you are praying, you are thanking God that he loves you, hears you, and will answer your prayer. You go before him because he is your loving daddy and he will answer you. And you walk tall throughout the day, without worrying about request.

5. **Focus on God instead of on circumstances.** *Isaiah 26:3[NLT]. You will keep in perfect peace all who trust in you, all whose thoughts are fixed on you. Finally, brothers, whatever is true, whatever is honorable, whatever is just, whatever is pure, whatever is lovely, whatever is commendable, if there is any excellence, if there is anything worthy of praise, think about these things. What you have learned and received and heard and seen in me – practice these things, and the God of peace will be with you.* (Philippians 4:8-9, ESV, emphasis added).

6. You overcome worry and anxiety by faith. You believe and confess that God is your loving Dad and He will always care for you. And enjoy your life by faith knowing your father cares. *Matthew 6:31. Acts 27:21-25.* Declare boldly today that; I refuse to worry and refuse to be anxious. I have the spirit of love, boldness and of a sound mind.

Day 19: *Victorious thought for the day.* I shall not be governed by worry and anxiety because God has not given me the spirit of fear but of power, love and a sound mind.

PRAYERS

I boldly declare that I refuse to worry and refuse to be anxious. I have the spirit of love, boldness and of a sound mind.

Luke 1:37. For with God nothing is impossible. Father, throughout this season, let nothing be impossible for me. Whatever will be assigned to me to do, I receive your uncommon grace to do them in Jesus name.

Psalms 91:5-6. You shall not be afraid of the terror by night, Nor of the arrow that flies by day, Nor of the pestilence that walks in darkness, Nor of the destruction that lays waste at noonday.

No power of darkness shall rule over my life and my family in Jesus name.

Every arrow coming from any unexpected or unsuspected area, unnoticed arrows, arrows flying beyond the region of spiritual sensitivity, begin to all catch fire, in Jesus name.

Every demonic spirit sent to cause me repeated pain and hurt, are arrested and sent back.

The terror by night and destruction of the wasters at noonday shall not locate me. It shall not locate any member of Abundant Life.

In this season; I announce no losses, no calamity, no evil occurrence in my life and family in Jesus name.

From this season and beyond, only news of joy will be my portion. Any power set to crush my life, I send them to the cross. Instead of crown of trouble, I receive the crown of favor and mercy. Every arrow of the wicked has missed me and my loved ones, in the name of Jesus

Luke 1:37. For with God nothing is impossible. Father, throughout this season, let nothing be impossible for me. Whatever will be assigned to me to do, I receive your uncommon grace to do them in Jesus name.

Day 20

ALL THINGS ARE NOW READY: MY SEASON OF SUPERNATURAL PROVISION

DAY 20
ALL THINGS ARE NOW READY: MY SEASON OF SUPERNATURAL PROVISION

Luke 14:16-17. Then said he unto him, A certain man made a great supper, and bade many. And sent his servant at supper time to say to them that were bidden, Come; for all things are now ready.

2 Kings 3:9,15-17, 20. So the king of Israel went, and the king of Judah, and the king of Edom: and they fetched a compass of seven days' journey: and there was no water for the host, and for the cattle that followed them. ⁵ *But now bring me a minstrel. And it came to pass, when the minstrel played, that the hand of the Lord came upon him.* ¹⁶ *And he said, Thus saith the Lord, Make this valley full of ditches.* ¹⁷ *For thus saith the Lord, Ye shall not see wind, neither shall ye see rain; yet that valley shall be filled with water, that ye may drink, both ye, and your cattle, and your beasts. Vs 20.* ²⁰ *And it came to pass in the morning, when the meat offering was offered, that, behold, there came water by the way of Edom, and the country was filled with water.*

This is your season of supernatural provision. God has gone ahead to make provisions for the journey. *Psalms 90:1-2.* Meaning before the problems, the solutions were already there. Everything you need materially has been provided for. In *Genesis 15:13-14,* God told Abraham prophetically about his seed going to a foreign land for 400 years in bondage and that he will bring them out with great substance. So when we read Exodus 12:36 and see the Israelites leaving with great substance, we need to understand that their deliverance came even before the bondage.

Before the crowd was hungered and fed by Jesus in *Mark 14:13-16*, God made provision by allowing the little boy to be in the crowd with his lunch.

In the encounter in 2 Kings 3, there was neither rain nor wind, but the valley was filled with water. This speaks of supernatural supplies. All things are now ready. Salvation is an invitation for supernatural provision. No matter what you are looking for in life, it is available. Everything you need for your flourishing has been prepared; everything you need for your manifestation is ready.

It is not enough that it has been provided for you, you have to take it.

HOW DO I CONNECT?

1. First thing is that a supernatural supply is a reality. It exists. God is a God of supernatural supplies. Since he exists in the supernatural, he is a God of supernatural provision. In *Luke 14:17*, God already made the provisions and invited everyone but several responses. Some were unwilling invitee. They came up with all kinds of excuses. *Isaiah 1:19*. Some were antagonistic invitees. *2 Kings 7:1-2*. But you must know and be willing. By redemption privilege, you are not permitted for your sweat to be responsible for everything. You are not permitted for your certificate to be responsible for everything. If everything you get in life comes from your certificate and your sweat, then your life is natural, ordinary and normal. Looking through the scripture The widow of Seraphite. Also *2 Kings 4:1-5. 1 Kings 17:4*, Abraham in *Genesis 22*. A ram caught in the ticket. The ram was going but God arrested it by the horn.

Peter in *Luke 5:1-5. Matthew 17:27*. Money in the mouth of the fish. Wine was finished but he asked them to pour water and it turned to wine. *John 2:1-7*. Everything was literally waiting for him everywhere. In this new season, you will see provisions you did not sweat for. This is your season to build houses and business and flourish supernaturally.

2. Connect with God and submit to prophetic mantle. *Psalms 23:1*. God must be your shepherd, so you do not live a life of lack and want. You must be a good son and daughter in the Lord. Do not exist as an average Christian. Do not play games with your salvation; rather, be properly connected with God in an intimate manner. Ensure that you are guided by appropriate pastoral cover/prophetic mantle. You must value and be in accordance with prophetic instructions. *2 Chronicles 20:20*. Your provision and prosperity is tied to the divine utterances of your prophet. In *John 2*, when they needed wine, Jesus instructed them to fill water pots with water. It was through that act of obedience - without any prayer - that water turned into wine.

3. Connect through the power of praise and thanksgiving. Child of God, this is not the season of sorrow, grumbling and complaining. It is your season of praise and thanksgiving. *Isaiah 12:3*. *With joy you will draw water from the wells of salvation*. Elisha said, bring me a minstrel and the direction came for supplies 2 Kings 3:15. The unction for multiplication in the kingdom is released through the vehicles of appreciation. Psalms 67:5. Supernatural supplies never answer to murmuring and grumbling.

4. Faith expectation actions. It is not just enough to know that all things are now ready. It is not just enough to know that God has made provisions for your manifestations, you must be willing to step out in faith actions. Elisha told the widow in 2 Kings 4 to go and borrow vessels. In 2 Kings 3,

they were told to dig the ditches and pour water. For every supernatural manifestation, there must be a natural initiation. Human expectation is the provoker of divine manifestations. There are things you do to let God know that you are thinking large.

5. Supernatural provision is embraced on the platform of offering and sacrifice. It is not possible to see supernatural supplies until you understand the power of offering and sacrifice. Before they could get wine, they had to give water. Before feeding the five thousand, there had to be the release of five loaves and fishes. *2 Kings 3:20*. When the meat offering was offered, then, behold, there came water. Until the meat offering was offered, there was no water. It does not matter who prophesied to you; so long you are stingy to God and his work, supernatural supplies will not be forthcoming. If you do not believe in tithing and prophetic giving, you can experience supernatural provision.

Day 20: *Victorious thought for the day.* Your provisions are not tied to the economy of the land you live but tied to your covenant with God. The economy of the land may fail, your covenant will never fail.

PRAYERS

Since the Lord is my shepherd, I shall not want and will never lack.

By the power of the cross, I connect with the Holy Spirit to lead me into the prepared blessings and prepared places ordained for my life.

From today, I will not walk in confusion and darkness; my eyes are open to divine provisions.

In this season of supernatural provision, I receive divine favor that destiny helpers will use their resources to advance my destiny in all areas in Jesus name.

Father, I receive the grace to honor you with my life, with my resources and be a channel of distribution of your wealth on the earth.

My father, my father, let every devourer coming against me be rebuked and destroyed in Jesus name.

Day 21

I AM POSITIONED FOR UNLIMITED HARVEST: THROUGH THANKSGIVING

DAY 21
I AM POSITIONED FOR UNLIMITED HARVEST: THROUGH THANKSGIVING

We are grateful for God's goodness and faithfulness since the beginning of this divine exercise. As you are coming to the end, you must position yourself for unlimited harvest through thanksgiving.

NOTE:

1. **Your degree of gratitude determines your degree of greatness in life.** It is your gratitude that determines your altitude. The more grateful you are, the more colorful your destiny becomes. One of the lessons we learn from the parable of the talents in *Luke 19* was gratitude. The person with one talent was ungrateful. The one given five and two were grateful with what they were given and utilized it wisely. As a result, they were given authority over more cities, which is dominion.
2. **Nothing benefits God directly like your thanksgiving.** The only thing God cannot do is to praise himself. That is why he is around those who praise and thank him.
3. **When you are thankful for what God has done for you, it qualifies you for more.** If you cannot see anything he

has performed, you are disqualified from receiving more from God. In the natural, when you show favor to anyone who does not respond with gratitude, you are constrained from doing any other favor for such a person. Whenever we take God for granted, we are grounded. Many Christians are grounded today because they take God for granted by complaining and murmuring. *1 Corinthians 10:10*. God cannot stand the look of those who murmur and complain..

4. **The right attitude of gratitude as a way of life is the magnet to draw God to yourself.** Ingratitude says God is incapable. It is casting aspersions on the personality and the integrity of God.
5. **Thanksgiving is far more potent than prayers**. Some people pray fervently, but they do not give thanks enthusiastically. When you pray, God hears you; when you thank him, he comes down. He comes down to see the operation himself. You can pray amiss, but cannot thank God amiss. David thanked his way into the heart of God. David praised and thanked God seven times daily, and prayed three times a day. *Psalms 119:164. Seven times a day do I praise thee because of thy righteous judgments.* No wonder he became a man after God's own heart.

WHAT IS THANKSGIVING?

Thanksgiving focuses on God's act while praise focuses on his personality. You give thanks for his acts and praise for his personality. This is the season to begin to thank God for this journey and the tremendous outcomes both now and in the future.

Thanksgiving appreciates God for what he has done, and praise appreciates God for who he is.

Thanksgiving and praise combined, stimulate God to do three things:

- It reminds God of who he is.
- It reminds God of what he has done before.
- And it moves God to repeat what he has done before.

WHAT HAPPENS WHEN YOU GIVE THANKS?

1. **You attract divine presence.** It invokes divine presence into a man's life. *Psalms 22:3*. Divine presence makes all the difference.
2. When you are committed to thanksgiving, **you attract unsolicited favor**. *Mark 6:21-36*. Ask me anything to the half of my kingdom. Favor landed on Herodias daughter because of thanksgiving. Nothing pleases God than your thanksgiving and praise. Dancing to the pleasure of the king brought favor to her. Imagine what comes your way when you dance to please the king of kings. It is unspeakable favor
3. **Thanksgiving is a catalyst for divine manifestations**. There is no spiritual force that is more potent that the force of thanksgiving. It is a catalyst that attracts the divine power of God for miraculous occurrences. When thanksgiving becomes your way of life, signs and wonders become your natural experience. *Psalms 67:5-6. Let the people praise thee, O God; let all the people praise thee. Then shall the earth yield her increase; and God, even our own God, shall bless us.*
4. **Thanksgiving releases fresh oil upon your life**. (Fresh anointing). *Psalms 92:10-11. But my horn shall thou exalt like the horn of a unicorn: I shall be anointed with fresh oil. Mine eye also shall see my desire on mine enemies, and mine ears shall hear my desire of the wicked that rise up against me.* Thanksgiving and praise guarantee fresh oil. God will empower

me with fresh oil to deal with my enemies. God will empower me with fresh oil to crush my opposition.

The job in your hands today, God gave it to you.

The life that makes it possible to do that job, God gave you.

That God is the reason for the results that we see.

God is the reason for the blessings that we enjoy.

God is the reason for the breath in our nostrils.

God is the reason for the food on our tables.

God is the reason for the peace in our families.

God is the reason for everything for the things people applaud us for.

MAINTAINING A LIFE OF CONTINUOUS THANKSGIVING

Psalms 103:1-5 NKJV Bless the Lord , O my soul; And all that is within me, bless His holy name! Bless the Lord , O my soul, And forget not all His benefits: Who forgives all your iniquities, Who heals all your diseases, Who redeems your life from destruction, Who crowns you with loving-kindness and tender mercies, Who satisfies your mouth with good things, So that your youth is renewed like the eagle's.

1. Count the blessings of redemption - John 3:16. Salvation is the most precious commodity in heaven and on earth.
2. Deliverance from danger - every human being has experienced deliverance from danger in a world filled with evil - Lord's prayer.
3. Mercy and kindness. Lamentations 3:23.
4. Divine satisfaction with good things (Divine nourishment)
5. Continuous strength.

HOW DO YOU COUNT YOUR BLESSINGS?

1. Having personal reflection. *Psalm 90:12.*
2. You need to keep personal blessing memorial.
3. Constant worship and appreciation to God.
4. Devoting your life as a testimony to His goodness.

Day 21: *Victorious thought for the day.* The cheapest way to experience unlimited manifestations is to recognize that God is the reason that you and I are alive.

PRAYERS

In the name of Jesus, I appreciate you, father, for the grace for this journey, for the grace to seek you daily, for the grace of fellowship with you and for the grace of salvation.

Thank you father for your goodness and provisions for me daily and always

I thank and appreciate you for speedy answers to all my prayers in this season and always in Jesus name.

I pray that the breakthroughs you have secured shall be permanent. That the open heavens you have secured shall remain opened. That there shall be testimonies of your spiritual labor. As the redeemed of the Lord you will return with your testimony.

Isaiah 51:11. I thank you father that there shall be testimonies of my spiritual labor. As the redeemed of the Lord, I will return with your testimony. As the redeemed of the Lord, I shall return with singing. I shall return with joy and gladness, and sorrow and mourning shall forever flee away from my life, in Jesus name.

As you end this adventure, set times aside to declare praise and thanksgiving to God. You have done several days of praying; it is now time to observe several days of praising and thanking

God. What do you do when you have done all? Keep praising and thanking God until your desires are accomplished.

Do not allow the enemy to steal your joy and your harvest. Keep watering your prayers with your thanksgiving. When it seems as if the manifestations are not coming as you expect them, keep your channel open by praising and thanking God. He is faithful to his work. You shall return with singing. You shall return with joy and gladness. Sorrow and mourning shall forever flee away from your life. I am awaiting your testimonies.

DAILY BREAKTHROUGH PRAYER POINTS

1. *Haggai 2:9.* The glory of this latter house shall be greater than of the former, saith the Lord of hosts: and in this place will I give peace, saith the Lord of hosts. *Revelation 21:4.* And God shall wipe away all tears from their eyes; and there shall be no more death, neither sorrow, nor crying, neither shall there be any more pain: for the former things are passed away. By the power in the name of Jesus, I say bye-bye, to the shame of the former times. Bye-bye, to the sorrows of the past; bye-bye, to the delays and afflictions of the past. Bye-bye, to the tragedies of the past. By the word of the Lord, affliction will never rise again in my life. This is my season of victory, abundance, and total breakthroughs.
2. In *Numbers 16*, Moses spoke to the ground, commanding it to open up and swallow his enemies, and God honored his word. Point your finger to the ground. Enemies of my fruitfulness and my manifestations; I bury you today and forever. Barrenness in whatever form, I bury you today and forever. Poverty and failure, I bury you today and forever. The spirit of stagnation and non-achievement, I bury you today and forever. *Matthew 16:18.*

3. *Ecclesiastes 7:10 [Ampl.]* "Do not say, Why were the old days better than these? For it is not wise or because of wisdom that you ask this." You are destined for a progressive destiny. In the name of Jesus, I pray that never will my previous year be better than the current year. I pray that every-day of my life will forever be better than the previous. In my career, in my business, in my finances, I shall experience ever increasing progress in Jesus name. I command my current season to be better, richer, overflowing with grace, overflowing with laughter, and overflowing with blessing, in the name of Jesus.
4. *Nehemiah 4:11.* And our adversaries said, "They shall not know, neither see, till we come in the midst among them, and slay them, and cause the work to cease." God will deliver you from invisible battles you do not know. *Ephesians 6:12.* Any invisible power that wants to cause the work of your hand to cease, is destroyed and returned to the sender. Every invisible arrow of the adversary meant to destroy my destiny is returned to sender in Jesus name.
5. *Genesis 35:16-18.* And they journeyed from Bethel; and there was but a little way to come to Ephrath: and Rachel travailed, and she had hard labor. And it came to pass, when she was in hard labor, that the midwife said unto her, Fear not; thou shalt have this son also. And it came to pass, as her soul was in departing, (for she died) that she called his name Benoni: but his father called him Benjamin." The Hebrew meaning of Ephrath is a fruitful place. A place of fruitfulness. Rachel died just a little distance from her place of fruitfulness. She was to finally deliver; finally follow her husband home; finally escape from the wickedness of her father; but she died shortly before getting to the end. Heavenly father, I pray and declare that I will not faint at my place of fruitfulness. I will not breakdown at a short distance from my breakthrough. I will not

breakdown at a short distance from my testimony. By the word of the Lord, I will reach my destiny's goal. The forces of breakdown at the edge of breakthrough are shattered forever in my life, in Jesus name.

6. *Psalms 51:8. "Make me to hear joy and gladness; that the bones which thou hast broken may rejoice."* This very day and season, I will hear good news concerning every area of my life. I will hear good news concerning my family. I will hear good news from my destiny helpers. I will receive letters, emails and texts bearing good news to my household in Jesus name.

7. *1 Kings 8:15.* Father, I pray that your prophetic mandate for my life this season shall be fulfilled speedily in Jesus name. I pray that your promises and mandate for my household and your churches worldwide shall be fulfilled by your mighty hands this year, in Jesus name.

8. *Psalms 68:19.* By the authority in the name of Jesus, I pray and decree that every day of my life shall be fully loaded with financial breakthroughs, spiritual breakthroughs, career and marital breakthroughs.

9. Since you are the God of completion, I pray that every incomplete area of my life will be brought to perfect completion by your grace and favor, in Jesus name.

10. *Romans 8:32, Psalms 84:11, Psalms 68:19.* My father, my father, by the power of redemption, increase my greatness and encompass me with your goodness all around. By the authority of God's word, my family and I will attract good and favorable things from now and henceforth.

11. *Proverbs 3:27-28.* Whatever assigned miracles, blessings and breakthroughs that have left the hands of God for my life, shall be delivered without any delay in Jesus name. Every force or power hindering the manifestation and the delivery of my assigned blessings is rebuked now in the name of Jesus. Every good and precious thing I am due for

in this season of my life according to God's divine plan shall be delivered into my destiny.
12. My God that answers by fire, show up in my life to shatter every limitation and barrier against my fruitfulness in Jesus name. Whatever stands between me and my appointed places is shattered by the hand of Jehovah God in Jesus name.
13. *1 Peter 5:10 [NLT]*. Heavenly Father, by your mercy, let my destiny be restored, strengthened, supported, and brought to a firm foundation this season and beyond, in Jesus name.
14. Because I dwell in the secret place of the most high, no evil shall befall me, and no plague will come near my dwelling. Every weapon of darkness that may rise against me is shattered and returned to the sender, in Jesus name.
15. Since the Lord is my light and my salvation, I conquer the spirit of fear and terror in Jesus name. I pray that God will baptize me with the spirit of boldness.
16. Since darkness cannot overpower light, I pray and declare that nothing will cover the light of my destiny from full manifestation. No matter the darkness around, I receive the grace to arise and shine in the midst of the darkness.
17. By the authority in the name of Jesus, I pray and declare that I am an agent of transformation and of Godly influence in my household, church, community, city, nation, and the entire world.
18. By the power of divine favor; my destiny will experience unlimited, unstoppable and unhindered progress, in Jesus name. By the authority in the name of Jesus, every barrier standing between my next level of progress and me is shattered and removed.
19. *Jeremiah 30:19. Isaiah 69:22. 2 Chronicles 26:15*. Father, grant me the grace to enjoy your divine help like never before in Jesus name. My father, my father, by your divine help my

destiny will not diminish or reduce but shall be multiplied and increase in good things.
20. *2 Kings 7:4-8.* I pray that my eyes of understanding are opened to receive strategies for profitable existence in Jesus name. Since God is my Shepherd, I shall be led daily into divinely prepared blessings and be led away from calamities and troubles.
21. By the authority in the name of Jesus, I pray that God will position men and women into my life who will use their resources, positions and wealth to forcefully advance my destiny. My destiny will never lack both divine and human support in Jesus name. By the grace of God I shall be a destiny helper to people and to his kingdom in Jesus name.

THE GREATEST PRAYER OF ALL TIME

The greatest prayer of a lifetime is to be reconnected back to God in a living relationship. Relationship is the basis for asking. You cannot pray to a God who you do not know and who does not know you. God wants to be intimate with you. This type of relationship is available to each one of us when we sincerely repent of our sins, ask for God's forgiveness, and receive His Son, Jesus, as our personal Lord and Savior. If you have never surrendered your life to God, or if you have turned away from God and you want to return to Him, now is the time. God is waiting for you. His arms are open wide to receive you. Just pray this simple prayer right now:

"O Lord, be merciful to me, a sinner. I realize that I am a sinner. I need a savior and you are my savior. I repent of every sin, every wrongdoing, and I ask for your forgiveness. I receive Jesus Christ, Your only begotten Son, as my Lord and my Savior. I believe that Jesus went to the cross for me and paid the price for my salvation, and now I receive Him into my heart. I declare that I am born again. I am a child of God. Old sins are gone, and I have a brand-new life in Christ, in Jesus Name. Amen."

NOTES

NOTES

NOTES

NOTES

www.ingramcontent.com/pod-product-compliance
Lightning Source LLC
LaVergne TN
LVHW051101080426
835508LV00019B/1997